THE MINISTRY OF HEALING

STUDY GUIDE

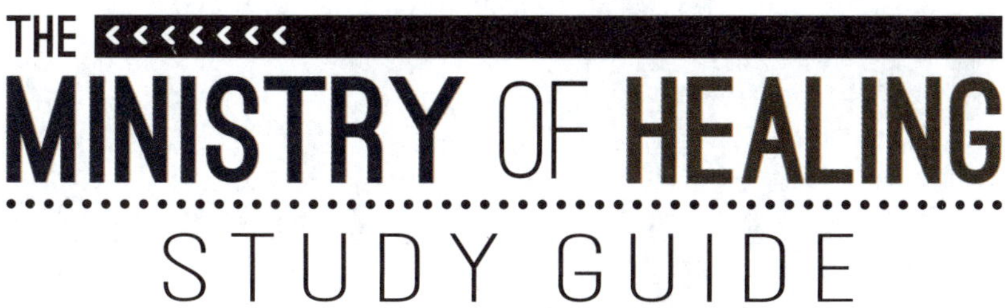

JON PAULIEN

Nampa, Idaho | Oshawa, Ontario, Canada
www.pacificpress.com

ADVENTIST HEALTH MINISTRIES | NORTH AMERICAN DIVISION
A PROJECT OF THE NORTH AMERICAN DIVISION HEALTH MINISTRIES

Cover and interior design by Aaron Troia
Cover design and interior resources from Thinkstock.com

The author assumes full responsibility for the accuracy of all facts and quotations as cited in this book.

You can obtain additional copies of this book by calling toll-free 1-800-765-6955 or by visiting http://www.adventistbookcenter.com.

ISBN 978-0-8163-5888-5

March 2016

CONTENTS

DEDICATION

I would like to dedicate this book to the faculty of the School of Religion at Loma Linda University. These studies are an outgrowth of our faculty discussions on *The Ministry of Healing* from January 2012 through January 2014. Thanks to these discussions, the "Thoughts" section of each chapter is many times richer than anything I would have thought of on my own. I am privileged to be part of this small community. Special acknowledgement goes to Ted Levterov, director of the White Estate Branch Office at Loma Linda University, who provided more than a third of the study questions for this book.

OUR EXAMPLE

CH. 1, PP. 17–28

SUMMARY

Jesus came (among other things) to model what we can and should be like.

Our mission is to continue the healing and teaching ministry of Jesus in today's world, the one that we experience.

THOUGHTS

Ellen White opens the chapter by summarizing the entire human condition in a simple phrase: "man's necessity." This singular word *necessity* includes within it all the ravages of disease and sin that Jesus came to undo. He came to provide humanity "health and peace and perfection of character."

Jesus' mission was to show the world what God (His Father) was like.

Our mission is to show the world what Jesus is like, so they can know what God is like.

Jesus "came not to destroy, but to save." This tells us about the fundamental attitude of God toward the human race. God is not arbitrary, quick to punish, abusive, as some make Him out to be, rather God loves, seeks to save, and, in caring concern, desires to move us to the place that would be best for us.

Jesus lived a life of constant self-sacrifice, yet was not recognized or honored for it.

On page 20, Ellen White talks about using each work of healing to implant "divine principles" into the mind and soul. What divine principles? A list would have been helpful here. Perhaps there is a hint in what follows in this short paragraph. The healings were done to "incline the hearts of men to receive the gospel of His grace." What "divine principles" do you think she had in mind here?

It is easier for human beings to fall in love with their interpretations about the Bible than to actually take the Bible seriously. In Jesus we have an Interpreter who was in on the writings when they were written.

Christ humbled Himself in order to meet us where we are. Jesus kept it simple and used familiar analogies from everyday life. He identified with people's interests and happiness. He studied to reach out to both poor and rich. If Jesus "studied" how to meet people where they are, it must have been by observation. I suppose to some degree we need to become like the people we want to influence. How far do you think Jesus took this? How far should we?

How far did Jesus go in His commitment to diversity? Ellen White mentions the roughest, the most unpromising, those under Satan's control, publicans, Samaritans. The one group she does not mention is the religious elite of Jesus' day. What are some contemporary equivalents of these outcast groups in Jesus' day?

At the close is the intriguing statement, "Wherever hearts are open to receive the truth, Christ is ready to instruct them . . . He uses no parables."

One outcome of the reading of this chapter is the sense that Ellen White was more principled than practical. She talked about "divine principles," for example, but did not spell them out. This suggests that she did not try to control how people carried out the principles in day-to-day situations; she allowed freedom to apply and adapt the principles to new situations as they arose. Applying such an approach to her counsel keeps that counsel fresh and relevant.

QUOTABLE QUOTES

"It was heaven to be in [Jesus'] presence."

"During His ministry, Jesus devoted more time to healing the sick than to preaching. His miracles testified to the truth of His words, that He came not to destroy, but to save."

DURING HIS MINISTRY, JESUS DEVOTED MORE TIME TO HEALING THE SICK THAN TO PREACHING.

"The Saviour made each work of healing an occasion for implanting divine principles in the mind and soul."

"Often that which men had taught and written about the Scripture was put in place of the Scripture itself."

"He was the Majesty of heaven, but He humbled Himself to take our nature, that He might meet men where they were."

"While He ministered to the poor, Jesus studied also to find ways of reaching the rich."

"Christ recognized no distinction of nationality or rank or creed. . . . He made no difference between neighbors and strangers, friends and enemies. . . . He passed by no human being as worthless."

@TWEETS_OF_HEALING

It was #heaven 2 b in @Jesus' presence.

Jesus' mission was 2 show the world wt @God was like. Our mission is 2 show the #world what @Jesus is like.

During #His ministry, @Jesus devoted more time 2 #healing the sick than 2 preaching. What does that tell us abt @God?

It is easier 4 #human beings 2 fall n #love wt their interpretations of the Bible than 2 actually take the Bible seriously.

Wherever #hearts r open, @Jesus dsnt need 2 use parables.

DISCUSSION QUESTIONS

1. If Jesus came to model what we can and should be like, how do we accomplish that in practice?
2. Jesus' mission was to show the world what God (His Father) is like.

What picture of God do you see in this chapter and in the five chapters that follow? On page 18, Ellen White says that it was heaven to be in Jesus' presence. What does that tell us about God?

3. Christ humbled Himself to meet us where we are. Likewise we are to meet people where they are if we want to influence them. These points are strongly made in the chapter but without reference to Scripture. What Bible texts or principles would confirm the main points of this chapter?

DAYS OF MINISTRY

CH. 2, PP. 29-50

SUMMARY

The kingdom that Jesus brought is truly "not of this world." The focus of Jesus' ministry, therefore, was on simplicity, spirituality, self-sacrifice, dependence on God, and development of character, rather than on the values of the wider world: wealth, power, fame, self-importance, and outward display.

THOUGHTS

Jesus was not satisfied to be a wonder-worker or a healer of physical disease. He sought to turn people's minds from the earthly to the spiritual. How do you do that in the context of Loma Linda (both clinical and educational) or a commercial business?

Jesus' methods of ministry were in direct contrast to the religious leaders of His day. He did not seek to become famous or start a mega-church. He did not wear his "religiosity" like a badge. His method was to go about quietly and gently like the dawn.

Jesus' agenda was not overtly political. He did not commit Himself to overturn kingdoms. Nevertheless, His life of mercy and self-sacrifice was a direct challenge to all the ways humans seek to gain advantage over each other, including political, military, and economic means. The power of Jesus' kingdom was most clearly seen in the transformation of character. The things that are seen and temporal are of value to the degree that they express the unseen and the eternal. God works in ways that are often not discernable and not assessable.

"CHRIST CAME TO THE EARTH AND STOOD BEFORE THE CHILDREN OF MEN WITH THE HOARDED LOVE OF ETERNITY."

Jesus' greatness was seen, not so much in His miracles and spectacular accomplishments as in His attention to the little things, such as the care of children and outcasts. Is the focus of Adventist health care on buildings and equipment and fancy billboards consistent with this mission? Do we care more about buildings and equipment than scholarship and character development? Character is as important as knowledge and skills. Should we care so much about how our institutions (schools and hospitals) rank in relation to others?

A quote from Alfred North Whitehead may be instructive here: "Seek simplicity and then distrust it."

Ellen White offers an interesting ecological suggestion on pages 47, 48. She saw the diet offered at the feeding of the 5,000 as a lesson in simplicity. If people lived more simply, in harmony with the laws of creation, there would be enough resources to supply the whole human family. It is selfishness and indulgence of appetite that have led to the extreme inequalities in the world.

QUOTABLE QUOTES

"The Pharisees . . . proved their zeal for religion by making it the theme of discussion."

"Wealth or high position, costly equipment, architecture or furnishings, are not essential to the advancement of the work of God."

"The choicest productions of art possess no beauty that can compare with the beauty of character, which is the fruit of the Holy Spirit's working in the soul."

"Christ came to the earth and stood before the children of men with the hoarded love of eternity."

"In choosing men and women for His service, God does not ask whether they possess worldly wealth, learning, or eloquence. He asks, 'Do they walk in such humility that I can teach them My way?' "

"Let not your un-Christlike character misrepresent Jesus. Do not keep the little ones away from Him by your coldness and harshness. Never give them cause to feel that heaven would not be a pleasant place to them if you were there."

"If men today were simple in their habits, living in harmony with nature's laws, as did Adam and Eve in the beginning, there would be an abundant supply for the needs of the human family."

@TWEETS_OF_HEALING

The @Pharisees proved #zeal for #religion by making it theme of discussion.

@Jesus' "#kingdom," focusing on #simplicity, self-sacrifice & development of character, is in radical contrast 2 the values of the world.

@Jesus did not seek 2 bcome famous or start a mega-church.

@Jesus' #life of self-sacrifice was a direct challenge 2 all the ways humans seek 2 gain advantage over each other.

@Jesus' #gr8ness was seen not so much in #His miracles as in #His attention 2 the care of #children & outcasts.

It is self-centeredness that has led 2 the extreme inequalities in 2day's #world.

Wealth or high position, costly equipment, architecture or furnishings, r not essential 2 the advancement of the wrk of @God.

The choicest productions of art possess no beauty that cn compare wt the beauty of #character.

Nvr make #children think that heaven would b a dreary place if u were thr.

DISCUSSION QUESTIONS

1. Jesus sought to turn people's minds from the earthly (wealth, power, fame, self-importance, outward display) to the heavenly (simplicity, spirituality, self-sacrifice, dependence on God, development of character). How do you do this in practice; at home, at school, at work, at church? How do we develop such values in ourselves and others?
2. Jesus' greatness was seen in His care for the children and outcasts. Is the focus of Adventist health ministries on buildings, equipment, and cutting-edge advertising compatible with such a mission? How do we learn to care as much about character development as about infrastructure?
3. God's criterion in calling people for His service is, "Do they walk in such humility that I can teach them My way?" (page 37). How do we gain such humility? What picture of God do you see in this chapter?

WITH NATURE AND WITH GOD

CH. 3, PP. 51-58

SUMMARY

The secret of a life of power is found in communion with Scripture, self, nature, and nature's God.

THOUGHTS

What did Ellen White mean by a "life of power"? It is not clearly defined in the chapter, but we could take it as the ability to handle the kind of stress and people pressure Jesus faced without inner turmoil; an inner peace that generates personal energy and exudes encouragement toward others. No one ever carried more responsibility than Jesus or carried it with such a combination of peace, power, and compassion.

The key to Jesus' "power" was absorbing the content of Scripture and then meditating on it in the context of nature. (Today we might also talk about living our faith in the context of what we know from science.) Jesus lived, to a great degree, an outdoor life (in a climate similar to southern California).

Using nature, Jesus called people's thoughts from the artificial to the natural. What implications does this have in a world of artificial reality and computer graphics?

Page 56 has an interesting test case for the problem of suffering. Jesus could have intervened to save John the Baptist but He did not, even though it severely tested His own disciples' faith. Interestingly, Ellen White doesn't tell us why Jesus did this, she just describes how He acted to comfort the disciples. How relevant is this to patient care?

Lives devoted to others nevertheless need to turn aside from ceaseless activity and contact with human needs to seek retirement and spiritual recharge. The solution to the great need of the world is not unceasing effort, but more people willing to sacrifice and serve.

The theme of this chapter (communion with nature and God) connects with what some have called "mysticism." There are two main types of mysticism: a mysticism of communion (in which an individual draws closer to God yet retains their own individuality) and a mysticism of absorption (in which the mystic loses the self in the experience of God—like a drop of water falling into the ocean and being absorbed into the whole). Ellen White seems to favor the communion type in this chapter.

Expressing the summary statement above in other words, this chapter invites us to be biblio-centric, ego-centric (in the best possible sense of that phrase), eco-centric, and theo-centric. To limit oneself to one or two of the above would diminish one's wholeness. All four legs are needed in a solid spiritual foundation.

In her own life, Ellen White did not always experience the kind of power she is talking about here. For her this chapter was more of a prayer than a prescription. We should resist using this chapter as a checklist that will discourage others.

It seems that Jesus acquired inner strength through introspection and direct communion with God. Ellen White, by way of contrast, was often beset with negative thoughts in solitude and seemed to rise out of depression in preaching (communion with others). Likewise today, there are some people who find strength in introspection and others who find it in fellowship. People who write devotional material tend to write about spiritual life from the perspective of their own temperaments. This often leaves others out.

QUOTABLE QUOTES

"The Saviour's life on earth was a life of communion with nature and with God. In this communion He revealed for us the secret of a life of power."

"When Jesus said to His disciples that the harvest was great and the

USING NATURE, JESUS CALLED PEOPLE'S THOUGHTS FROM THE ARTIFICIAL TO THE NATURAL.

laborers were few, He did not urge upon them the necessity of ceaseless toil, but bade them, 'Pray ye therefore the Lord of the harvest, that He will send forth laborers into His harvest.' " Matthew 9:38.

"All who are under the training of God need the quiet hour for communion with their own hearts, with nature, and with God."

"When every other voice is hushed, and in quietness we wait before Him, the silence of the soul makes distinct the voice of God. He bids us, 'Be still and know that I am God.' " Psalm 46:10. This is the effectual preparation for all labor for God."

@TWEETS_OF_HEALING

The secret of a #life of #power is found in communion wt #Scripture, self, #nature & nature's @God.

@Jesus' #life combined, peace, humility & compassion wt "conscious power."

The key 2 @Jesus' "#power" was absorbing the content of #Scripture & then meditating on it in the context of #nature.

@Jesus lived, 2 a gr8 degree, an #outdoor #life (climate similar 2 southern California).

Using nature, @Jesus called ppl's thoughts frm the artificial 2 the natural. How do u do that in a world of virtual reality?

The solution 2 the gr8 need of the world isnt unceasing effort, bt more ppl willing 2 sacrifice & serve.

The #silence of the #soul makes distinct the voice of @God.

In communion we draw closer 2 @God wtout losing our own #individuality.

Some draw inner strength thru #introspection, others thru #connection wt ppl.

Ppl who write abt #spiritual #life tend 2 do so frm perspective of their own temperament & personality.

DISCUSSION QUESTIONS

1. What did Ellen White mean when she talked about a "life of power"? (page 51). How does one attain that kind of life? In her own life Ellen White did not always experience the kind of power she is talking about, her life was filled with illness, challenging people, and at times depression. How do you think she related to her own counsel here?
2. Using nature, Jesus called people's thoughts from the artificial to the natural (page 54). What implications does this have for a world of artificial reality and computer graphics?
3. Jesus could have intervened to save John the Baptist, but He did not, even though it severely tested the faith of His disciples (page 56). What implications does this have for treatment of the sick and suffering? What implications does it have for our picture of God?

THE TOUCH OF FAITH

CH. 4, PP. 59-72

SUMMARY

The key to connection with God is "the touch of faith." That means to reach out to God with a whole heart, out of great need, in growing trust, and with a deep sense of purpose.

THOUGHTS

Jesus was able to distinguish the touch of faith from the casual touch of a careless crowd. The woman touched Jesus with a "deep sense of purpose." I suppose the question is, To what degree is faith the central focus and concern in a person's life? Whole-hearted faith is powerful in our connection with God.

Faith is more than an opinion or an assent to certain ideas as truth, it is trust in a person that connects one into covenant relationship with God. It is a life-changing transaction.

Genuine faith makes humble people confident in spite of their sense of unworthiness. You can have confidence distrusting yourself, when your confidence is based on the mercy of God. God does not accept us because we are worthy, He accepts us because He promised to.

In some instances of healing, Jesus delayed granting the request, especially when it had to do with "earthly blessings." But He never delays granting requests for deliverance from sin.

We can trust ourselves to God because in the Elder Brother (Jesus), He knows by experience our weaknesses, our wants and needs, and the strength of our temptations. God "gets" us. And that makes it safe for us to "get" Him.

JESUS IS OPEN TO ALL KINDS OF PEOPLE.

There is a lot of research recently on the power of touch. Touch is a good health practice and promotes wholeness. Animals often go to the one who touches them more than the one who supplies food! Cornell has or recently had a masters degree in therapeutic touch. The Loma Linda community has a "Healing Hands" massage ministry.

In this chapter, the word *faith* is tied to many metaphors: touch, transaction, energy, purification, also legal and athletic (or pilgrim) metaphors. It is hard for human beings to get a handle on faith intellectually.

Is there a physiological aspect to faith? (Think wholeness.) Symbols and metaphors participate in the reality that they point to. All aspects of the person are intertwined.

The diversity of people in this chapter shows that Jesus is open to all kinds of people.

QUOTABLE QUOTES

"The faith that is unto salvation is not a mere assent to the truth of the gospel. True faith is that which receives Christ as a personal Saviour."

"Many hold faith as an opinion. Saving faith is a transaction, by which those who receive Christ join themselves in covenant relation with God. A living faith means an increase of vigor, a confiding trust, by which, through the grace of Christ, the soul becomes a conquering power."

"In working for the victims of evil habits, instead of pointing them to the despair and ruin toward which they are hastening, turn their eyes away to Jesus. Fix them upon the glories of the heavenly."

"The centurion said of himself, 'I am not worthy.' Yet he did not fear to ask help from Jesus. Not to his own goodness did he trust, but to the Saviour's mercy. His only argument was his great need."

"As you come to Him, believe that He accepts you, because He has promised. You can never perish while you do this—never."

"When we pray for earthly blessings, the answer to our prayer may be delayed, or God may give us something other than we ask, but not so when we ask for deliverance from sin."

"The Elder Brother of our race . . . knows by experience what are the weaknesses of humanity, what are our wants, and where lies the strength of our temptations."

"The weaker and more helpless you know yourself to be, the stronger you will become in His strength."

"Human love may change, but Christ's love knows no change."

@TWEETS_OF_HEALING

Mny hold #faith as an opinion, bt #saving #faith is a transaction.

U cn hve confidence thru #unworthy, when ur confidence is based on the #mercy of @God.

@God dsnt accept us b/c we r worthy, #He accepts us b/c He promised 2.

The heaviest #burden we carry is the burden of #sin.

@God "gets" us & that makes it #safe for us 2 "get" #Him.

The weakr & more helpless u know yrslf 2 b, the #stronger u will bcome n @God's "#strength."

Human #love may chng, bt #Christs #love knows no chng.

Better #Twinkies wt #love than #tofu wtout!

Is thr a physiological aspect 2 #faith? Symbols & meta4s participate n the reality that they pnt 2.

Its hrd 4 human bngs 2 get a hndl on #faith intellectually. Its more of an exp.

Animals often go 2 the 1 who touches them more tn the 1 who supplies food!

DISCUSSION QUESTIONS

1. What does Ellen White mean by "the touch of faith"? There has been

a lot of research into the power of touch recently. Animals often go to the one who touches them more than the one who provides food. How is it possible to reach out and "touch" God with a whole heart and a deep sense of purpose?

2. How does one come to God confidently and yet with a sense of unworthiness at the same time?
3. What picture of God do you see in this chapter?

HEALING OF THE SOUL

CH. 5, PP. 73-94

SUMMARY

A vital component of whole-person health care is conviction of sin and healing from "spiritual diseases" (or "renewing of the heart").

THOUGHTS

"Healing" and "salvation" are both translations of the same word in the Greek, thus providing a biblical foundation for the basic concept of this chapter.

Health care should not be made dependent on whether a person brought disease upon themselves or not. Jesus healed every person, regardless of their past and present vices. This point is also strongly illustrated by the story on page 91. Being in His presence, however, also brought conviction of sin and many were healed of "spiritual disease" as well as of their physical maladies. So it seems that spiritual healing is more conditional than physical healing is or should be.

The great condition of divine healing is a sense of need. God "fills the hungry with good things" and sends "the rich" away empty (Luke 1:53). How much more would God do in today's world were it not for a pride that knows no need?

The power to read the heart was evidence that Jesus had the power to forgive sins.

The root of healing power is creation power. The voice that brought something out of nothing and created humans from "dust" is capable of speaking life to dying bodies. And the same power that gives life to human bodies can also renew the heart, the spiritual and emotional side of the human condition. The question that plagues us, of course, is why this happens at some times (rarely?) and not others.

Jesus longs to exercise His healing power and make every sufferer whole. But circumstances alter cases. This may sometimes be related to the point of page 75, that we often get in the way of God's work for us. But in the Pool of Bethesda story it was political and contextual circumstances that prevented Jesus from doing more than He did on that occasion.

Remorse for sin is a major deterrent to wholistic health.

It is the Holy Spirit's job to convict of sin, so why this large emphasis in this chapter? It depends on the definition of sin. If you define sin in terms of separation from God, one can engage a patient to discover how they may have become separated from God, self, and others. Ellen White was not in favor of preaching fear and condemnation, so this is not what she meant in this chapter. She takes a larger view of sin in terms of alienation from God (breaking the law is a symptom of the deeper problem).

The rebuke of wrong-doing is certainly appropriate in some contexts (injustice, abuse), but the hospital setting is not a good place for that.

In many ways, language today is different from Ellen White's day. Instead of "sin" we may speak of brokenness or alienation, metaphors that are different from "sin" but also grounded in the biblical worldview.

If the quote on page 84 (see below) is true, we should avoid condemning a patient for what they are not capable of doing. We can point them instead to the power and graciousness of God.

It may be helpful to distinguish between sin and iniquity or lawlessness. Sin is a translated biblical term for "missing the mark." Everyone misses the mark sometimes. But iniquity or lawlessness is when one intends to miss the mark. Such versions of "sin" need to be confronted in the context of loving relationship.

QUOTABLE QUOTES

"Of ourselves we are no more capable of living a holy life than was the impotent man capable of walking."

"The greater the sinner's guilt, the more he needs the Saviour. His heart of divine love and sympathy is drawn out most of all for the one who is

ELLEN WHITE WAS NOT IN FAVOR OF PREACHING FEAR AND CONDEMNATION.

the most hopelessly entangled in the snares of the enemy. With His own blood He has signed the emancipation papers of the race."

"He does not tell to any all that He might reveal, but He bids every trembling soul take courage."

"There are multitudes today as truly under the power of evil spirits as was the demoniac of Capernaum. All who willfully depart from God's commandments are placing themselves under the control of Satan. Many a man tampers with evil, thinking that he can break away at pleasure; but he is lured on and on, until he finds himself controlled by a will stronger than his own."

"No cry from a soul in need, though it fail of utterance in words, will be unheeded."

"It is true that Satan is a powerful being; but, thank God, we have a mighty Saviour, who cast out the evil one from heaven. Satan is pleased when we magnify his power. Why not talk of Jesus? Why not magnify His power and His love?"

@TWEETS_OF_HEALING

The power 2 read the heart was evidence that @Jesus had the power 2 #forgive #sins.

The root of #healing #power is #creation #power.

The same power that gives #life 2 human bodies cn also renew the #heart.

@Jesus longs 2 exercise His #healing #power & make every sufferer whole. bt circumstances alter cases.

Of ourslvs we r no more capable of livng a holy #life tn was the impotent man at the #PoolofBethesda capable of walking.

Remorse 4 sin is a major deterrent 2 wholistic #health.

The gr8er the sinner's #guilt, the more he/she needs the @Saviour.

Wt #His own blood @Christ has signed the emancipation papers of the race.

#Spiritual #healing is more conditional than #physical #healing. The gr8 condition of divine #healing is a sense of need.

@Satan is pleased when we magnify his #power. Why not talk of @Jesus instead?

"Healing" & "salvation" r translations of same #Greek word.

"Sin" is missing the mark. "Lawlessness" is missing the mark on purpose.

When the arguments r weak, the righteous use force & ridicule.

#Adultery dsnt begin in bed, it ends in bed.

DISCUSSION QUESTIONS

1. According to this chapter, the root of healing power is creation power. The same God that brought something out of nothing can also speak life to sick and dying bodies. The question is: Why does this happen sometimes or even rarely and not at other times or all the time?
2. If it is the Holy Spirit's job to convict people of sin, why does Ellen White place so much emphasis in this chapter on helping people come to conviction of sin?
3. What picture of God do you see in this chapter?

SAVED TO SERVE

CH. 6, PP. 95-107

SUMMARY

Everyone who has benefitted from the saving ministry of Jesus is to share that experience with others. In this way we continue the teaching and healing ministry of Jesus in today's world.

THOUGHTS

This chapter was by far the richest treasure trove of quotable quotes so far. This theme must have been particularly meaningful to Ellen White herself. She seems to have been melancholy as a person and one way she kept her spirits up was in sharing the good things she had experienced with God with others by both pen and voice.

God's primary means of revealing Christ to the world is our testimony of God's faithfulness in our own lives. This is even more effective than teaching drawn directly from biblical sources. When people see the working of God's power in our lives, it has particular effect. Each person is unique and my witness to God's unique impact on my life can touch people that most others could not. When life and testimony are in harmony, there is a power present that impacts the salvation of others. This same power also impacts our own lives, drawing us nearer to Jesus in our own experience.

We are not to limit ministry to those who will honor us in their acceptance of it. The benefits of the gospel are to be shared freely with all. And this will be the natural tendency of those with a deep experience in spiritual things.

To the degree that we are people of privilege, whether that involves education, training, financial security, nobility of character, or religious experience, we owe a debt to those who are less favored in these things. Like the angels, who serve where they are most needed, we owe the most to those who are outcast, downtrodden, and inferior in education and character. Privilege calls us to minister in contexts the selfish heart would consider humiliating. In this we also follow the example of Jesus, who was rich and chose to become poor that we might be enriched through His poverty.

WHEN LIFE AND TESTIMONY ARE IN HARMONY, THERE IS A POWER PRESENT THAT IMPACTS THE SALVATION OF OTHERS.

Ellen White seems to believe that unselfish ministry of the love of Christ to others will have greater impact on social issues than the efforts of law courts and political (or military) action. How do we balance moral advocacy (social action) and personal concern for others?

Reading this chapter makes it clear that the community Ellen White was encouraging was not a gnostic-type community, a repository of secret knowledge. She urged that what the community knew and experienced be shared freely with all. In fact, she felt that our confession of God's faithfulness to us personally is critical to our healing ministry to others (see quote from page 100 below). And each of these testimonies is uniquely marked by our own individuality. So there is no cookie-cutter approach to witnessing, witnessing arises out of our experience. In other words, everyone can do what Ellen White recommends here, it doesn't require extensive training.

How does the Holy Spirit become real in the context of today's world? Through the actions of words of God's people, others see Jesus in simple gestures of kindness and caring concern. Expressions of kindness have a bigger impact than we realize.

The chapter makes frequent use of the word *missionary.* This term had much more positive implications in the nineteenth century than it does now. Today it sounds colonial and condescending to many people. So we may want to come up with different language to describe some of Ellen White's visions for service today.

QUOTABLE QUOTES

"The gospel is to be presented, not as a lifeless theory, but as a living force to change the life."

"Even those whose course has been most offensive to Him He freely accepts."

"We are to acknowledge His grace as made known through the holy men of old; but that which will be most effectual is the testimony of our own experience. . . . God desires that our praise shall ascend to Him, marked with our own individuality. These precious acknowledgments to the praise of the glory of His grace, when supported by a Christlike life, have an irresistible power that works for the salvation of souls."

"It is for our own benefit to keep every gift of God fresh in our memory. By this means faith is strengthened to claim and to receive more and more. There is greater encouragement for us in the least blessing we ourselves receive from God than in all the accounts we can read of the faith and experience of others."

"The gospel invitation is not to be narrowed down and presented only to a select few, who, we suppose, will do us honor if they accept it. The message is to be given to all. When God blesses His children, it is not alone for their own sake, but for the world's sake."

"He who drinks of the living water becomes a fountain of life. The receiver becomes a giver."

"It is in working to spread the good news of salvation that we are brought near to the Saviour."

"That we might become members of the heavenly family, He became a member of the earthly family."

"By all that has given us advantage over another,—be it education and refinement, nobility of character, Christian training, religious experience,—we are in debt to those less favored; and, so far as lies in our power, we are to minister unto them. If we are strong, we are to stay up the hands of the weak."

"He who was rich in heaven's priceless treasure became poor, that through His poverty we might be rich. We are to follow in the path He trod."

"Many feel that it would be a great privilege to visit the scenes of Christ's life on earth, to walk where He trod, to look upon the lake beside which He loved to teach, and the hills and valleys on which His eyes so often rested. But we need not go to Nazareth, to Capernaum, or to Bethany, in order to walk in the steps of Jesus. We shall find His footprints beside the sickbed, in the hovels of poverty, in the crowded alleys of the great cities, and in every place where there are human hearts in need of consolation."

"The love of Christ, manifested in unselfish ministry, will be more effective in reforming the evildoer than will the sword or the court of justice."

@TWEETS_OF_HEALING

The #gospel is not a #lifeless theory, it's a #living force 2 chng the #life.

@Jesus freely accepts even those whose choices in #life hve been the most offensive 2 #Him.

Whl #Bible teaching is extremely important, the most effectv teaching is the #testimony of our own exp wt @God.

@God desires that our praises will ascend 2 Him marked wt our own individuality.

Thr is more encouragement in the least blessing we receive frm @God than in all accounts of the #faith & exp of others.

The soul that responds 2 the #grace of @God is like a well-watered garden.

When one's #life & #testimony r in harmony, thr is a power present that impacts the #salvation of others.

Every #true #disciple is born into the kingdom of @God as a #missionary.

He who drinks of the #living water bcomes a fountain of #life. The receiver bcomes a giver.

It's in wrking 2 spread the good news of #salvation that we r brought near 2 the #Saviour.

@Jesus bcame a member of the earthly family, so we might bcome members of the #heavenly #family.

The more we hve, the more we owe 2 those who hve not.

@Jesus chose 2 b poor, so we cn bcome "rich."

@Jesus voluntarily left #heaven, so we cld hve the opt of going thr.

We cn walk 2day where @Jesus walked when we minister 2 the poor, the outcast, the depressed.

#Unselfish care for others will do more 2 #change the world positively than all of its courts & military power combined.

Ppl c @Jesus 2day in simple gestures of #kindness & caring concern.

Every1 who has benefited frm the saving #ministry of @Jesus is 2 share that exp wt others.

Thr is no cookie-cutter approach 2 witness, #witness arises out of our exp.

Expressions of #kindness hve a bigger impact than we realize.

Ppl often pursue the #healing professions out of their own #brokenness, bt they themselves find no healing thr.

DISCUSSION QUESTIONS

1. Ellen White seems to believe that unselfish ministry to others will have greater impact on social issues than the efforts of law courts and political action. How do we balance social action and personal concern for others?
2. According to this chapter, how does the Holy Spirit become real in the context of today's world?
3. What picture of God do you see in this chapter?

THE CO-WORKING OF THE DIVINE AND THE HUMAN

CH. 7, PP. 111-124

SUMMARY

Physicians themselves do not heal anyone. Their job is to help patients cooperate with the laws of nature and with God, who has implanted natural healing agencies in both body and mind. The greatest of these healing agencies is the gospel. When the gospel comes to a person, it frees mind and body from the anxiety, care, and guilt that crush the life forces.

THOUGHTS

This chapter expresses the point that the most effective healing ministry transcends the processes of nature by involving the healing power of Christ.

According to this chapter, disease is to a large degree entwined with sin. Every practice that destroys mental, physical, or spiritual energy is sin. Health is secured through obedience to God's laws. The Bible and science reveal the principles of life, the physician is to help others obtain a knowledge of these principles and, by obeying them, cooperate with God in the process of healing. This is very true, but needs to be qualified in our experience by the phrase "all other things being equal." All other things being equal, sin leads to disease and obedience leads to health (an expansion of the message of Proverbs). But in this life, things are not always equal. Living over a toxic waste dump without knowing it, for example, will undo all of one's careful obedience (sin is not just specific actions, it is a power that seeks to rule all of life). In this life, the wicked sometimes prosper and the righteous suffer and are impoverished. If we don't emphasize this, reading this chapter could be further discouraging to the sick and depressed.

Read without qualification, these pages could also lead to a mindless legalism. But Ellen White in this case does the qualification herself. On page 115, she points out that the gospel of free grace is the crucial healing principle. Principles to obey without the gospel discourage and depress, the gospel brings the serenity and composure that truly heal.

"Religion" is not just to be "value added" in the life and work of the physician, it is to be the influence that dominates all others.

Most patients will have more confidence in a physician if they know he or she is a believer. They realize their lives are in the hands of another and that one small human mistake could be fatal. When they know the physician is praying they have confidence that God is guiding the situation. Faith also brings quietness and courage to the physician.

Friends and family of the patient are often as wide open to spiritual care as the patient.

Cooperation with God is a key element of the perspective outlined in this chapter. It is a distinctly Adventist perspective, more akin to Calvin than Luther. Science has its limitations, but Ellen White teaches us to study science and religion together. As a rule, God works in and through the laws of nature. One exception to the rule might be the resurrection of Jesus.

Given the more secular nature of society today, we might want to nuance a bit some of the overt witnessing that this chapter implies. We need to balance our obligation to tell the truth with the needs and capacity of the patient.

If you want to do God's work, you will seek the highest medical qualifications you can.

For Ellen White, the term "natural remedies" was probably narrower in focus than it is today. By this phrase she was thinking of water treatments and herbs, which was radical thinking at the time. Similarly, telling people to stop smoking was radical at a time when physicians were prescribing smoking for the lungs!

QUOTABLE QUOTES

"Deliverance from sin and the healing of disease were linked together. The same ministry is committed to the Christian physician. He is to unite with Christ in relieving both the physical and spiritual needs of his fellow men."

"That which physicians can only aid in doing, Christ accomplishes. They endeavor to assist nature's work of healing; Christ Himself is the healer. The physician seeks to preserve life; Christ imparts life."

"Sickness, suffering, and death are work of an antagonistic power. Satan is the destroyer; God is the restorer."

"Men need to learn that the blessings of obedience, in their fullness, can be theirs only as they receive the grace of Christ. It is His grace that gives man power to obey the laws of God. It is this that enables him to break the bondage of evil habit."

"Not all this world bestows can heal a broken heart, or impart peace of mind, or remove care, or banish disease. Fame, genius, talent—all are powerless to gladden the sorrowful heart or to restore the wasted life. The life of God in the soul is man's only hope."

"The love which Christ diffuses through the whole being . . . frees the soul from the guilt and sorrow, the anxiety and care, that crush the life forces."

"The physician who is satisfied with a low standard of skill and knowledge not only belittles the medical profession, but does dishonor to Christ, the Chief Physician."

"The Physician should gather to his soul the light of the word of God. He should make continual growth in grace. With him, religion is not to be merely one influence among others. It is to be an influence dominating all others."

"If the golden opportunity is not watched for, it will be lost. At the bedside of the sick no word of creed or controversy should be spoken. Let the sufferer be pointed to the One who is willing to save all that come to Him in faith. Earnestly, tenderly strive to help the soul that is hovering between life and death."

"The same power that Christ exercised when He walked visibly among men is in His word."

"The Scriptures are to be received as God's word to us, not written merely, but spoken."

@TWEETS_OF_HEALING

Deliverance frm sin & the healing of #disease r linked 2gether.

The #physician seeks 2 preserve #life; @Christ imparts life.

@Satan is the destroyer, @God is the #restorer.

All other things being equal, the way of @God's #commandments is the way of #life.

Not all this #world bestows cn heal a broken #heart, or impart #peace of mind, or remove care, or banish #disease.

Fame, genius & talent r all powerless 2 restore a wasted #life, the power of @God is our only #hope.

The #love of @Christ frees the soul frm the guilt & sorrow, the anxiety & care, that crush the #life forces.

In whole-person care, #religion is not 1 influence among others, it's 2 b the influence dominating all others.

At the #bedside of the sick no #word of creed or controversy should b spoken.

The same #power that @Christ exercised when #He walked visibly among men is in #His #word.

The #Scriptures r 2 b received as @God's #word 2 us, not written merely, bt spoken.

Oldster overheard recently: When it comes 2 my body, if it dsnt hurt, it no longer wrks!

DISCUSSION QUESTIONS

1. According to this chapter, health professionals themselves do not heal anyone. Their job is to help patients cooperate with the laws of nature and with God. How does one do this in practice? How does one apply this principle to one's own life?
2. How in practice can busy health professionals help their patients obtain a knowledge of the principles of health that they have learned from the Bible and science?
3. Ellen White says that at the bedside "no word of creed or controversy should be spoken" (page 120). How does one apply this counsel when the patient is a Jew, a Muslim, or even an atheist?

THE PHYSICIAN, AN EDUCATOR

CH. 8, PP. 125–136

SUMMARY

The true physician is an educator. But it is the practice of the principles the physician teaches that gives them weight. True physicians recognize their responsibility, not only to the sick under their care, but also to the community in which they live. The responsibility of the physician to patients is not only for this life, but also for eternity.

THOUGHTS

The godly physician has the responsibility not only to educate the patient but also the community in which he or she lives. The education involves prevention as well as treatment.

In educating to healthful principles, physicians will find themselves battling the artificiality of civilization, custom, fashion, laziness, and the desire for short-term comfort over long-term health.

How should we best relate to statements such as "drugs do not cure diseases" and "health is recovered in spite of the drug"? Is that still true today or have "drugs" changed? Drugs certainly have changed over the last one hundred years. Later in her life, Ellen White did accept some pharmaceutical drugs. But in Ellen White's day, especially early on, drugs were often poisons (smoking and arsenic are examples of common remedies back then). We use hardly any of the nineteenth-century drugs today. Today's pharmaceuticals work better and we understand their effects better. Some of them are absolutely amazing in their life-saving and life-enhancing ability (insulin and antibiotics are excellent examples). At the same time, we should not replace the principles of healthy living with the promises of "Big Pharma." Negative interactions among drugs and between drugs and natural remedies (like vitamin supplements) suggest taking as few as possible of both in the context of a healthy diet and lifestyle.

Ellen White says that health does not depend on chance but is the result of obedience to law. Is this always true or is there a qualifier we need to add today?

An important reason for healthful living is that the lessening of physical vigor has repercussion in the moral and spiritual realm, making it harder to discriminate between right and wrong and more difficult to resist evil. The body is the only medium through which God can communicate to build up the character. The passions are to be controlled by the will, which itself is under the control of God. Interestingly, the ideas summarized in this paragraph were very common in the writings of Wesley (with whom Ellen White was very familiar) and before him, Thomas Aquinas.

Physicians can only have the strength to meet their arduous responsibilities if they take care of their own health first and also rely on God's presence and power.

One point that is often missed today is that Ellen White strongly identified with the social reform movements of her day. Language from those social reforms permeates this chapter and a true application of the chapter will also consider the social implications of her writings in today's world.

QUOTABLE QUOTES

"The true physician is an educator. He recognizes his responsibility, not only to the sick who are under his direct care, but also to the community in which he lives."

"Our artificial civilization is encouraging evils destructive of sound principles. Custom and fashion are at war with nature."

"Many transgress the laws of health through ignorance, and they need instruction. But the greater number know better than they do. They need to be impressed with the importance of making their knowledge a guide of life."

"When attacked by disease, many will not take the trouble to search out the cause of their illness. Their chief anxiety is to rid themselves of pain and inconvenience."

"Pure air, sunlight, abstemiousness, rest, exercise, proper diet, the use of water, trust in divine power—these are the true remedies. Every person should have a knowledge of nature's remedial agencies and how to apply them."

"The use of natural remedies requires an amount of care and effort that many are not willing to give. Nature's process of healing and upbuilding is gradual, and to the impatient it seems slow. The surrender of hurtful indulgences requires sacrifice. But in the end it will be found that nature, untrammeled, does her work wisely and well. Those who persevere in obedience to her laws will reap the reward in health of body and health of mind."

"Too little attention is generally given to the preservation of health. It is far better to prevent disease than to know how to treat it when contracted. It is the duty of every person, for his own sake, and for the sake of humanity, to inform himself in regard to the laws of life and conscientiously to obey them."

"Whatever injures the health, not only lessens physical vigor, but tends to weaken the mental and moral powers. Indulgence in any unhealthful practice makes it more difficult for one to discriminate between right and wrong, and hence more difficult to resist evil. It increases the danger of failure and defeat."

"Nothing with which we have to do is small. Every act casts its weight into the scale that determines life's victory or defeat."

"While, on the one hand, danger lurks in a narrow philosophy and a hard, cold orthodoxy, on the other hand there is great danger in a careless liberalism."

"The physician who ministers in the homes of the people, watching at the bedside of the sick, relieving their distress, bringing them back from the borders of the grave, speaking hope to the dying, wins a place in their confidence and affection, such as is granted to few others. . . . The physician's example, no less than his teaching, should be a positive power on the right side. The cause of reform calls for men and women whose life practice is an illustration of self-control. It is our practice of the principles we inculcate that gives them weight."

@TWEETS_OF_HEALING

The true #physician is an #educator.

Our #artificial civilization is encouraging evils destructive of sound principles. Custom & fashion r at war wt #nature.

When attacked by #disease, rther than search out the cause of their #illness many wish only 2 rid themselves of #pain & inconvenience.

Pure air, sunlight, abstemiousness, rest, exercise, proper diet, the use of water, trust in #divine power—these r the true remedies.

The use of #natural remedies requires an amount of care & effort that many r not willing 2 give.

It is far better 2 prevent #disease than 2 know how 2 treat it.

#Healthful #living avoids the extremes of hard, cold orthodoxy & careless #liberalism.

By becoming 1 wt @Christ, man is made free. Subjection 2 the will of @Christ means restoration 2 perfect #manhood.

It's our #practice of the principles we teach that gives them weight.

Many recover #health only 2 repeat the indulgences that invited #disease.

DISCUSSION QUESTIONS

1. How should we best relate today to statements such as "drugs do not cure diseases" and "health is recovered in spite of the drug"? Are these statements still true or have "drugs" changed?
2. How can physicians find the time and strength to take care of their own health first, in order to be more effective with their patients? How can they build a sense of God's presence and power into every element of their practice?

TEACHING AND HEALING

CH. 9, PP. 139–160

SUMMARY

In the work of the gospel, teaching and healing should never be separated. The wholeness of human beings requires wholeness of ministry.

THOUGHTS

On page 144, Ellen White says that the object of medical missionary work is to point people to the Man of Calvary. We are to encourage the sick and the suffering to look to Jesus and live. But this was written at a time when American culture was truly Christian. How is it different today?

On page 147 (see the quotes that follow on the next page), Ellen White notes that as institutions get bigger and bigger, the employees tend to excuse themselves from serious contact with the world and become self-absorbed. If she were alive today, would she say that Loma Linda University (or any other Adventist institution) is too big in the context of today's world? Or are things different today than in her day? Big doesn't necessarily mean detached from personal effort or self-absorbed, but it does require institution-wide effort and attention. In today's world, large institutions can have a large impact on communities and the wider culture. All other things being equal, it is easier to be faithful when you are small, but a large and faithful institution can accomplish great things in the world. But where institutions become a substitute for personal effort, they may do more harm than good.

Although teaching and healing are to be combined, Christ's method is

CHRIST'S METHOD IS NOT TO HAMMER PEOPLE WITH TEACHINGS THEY ARE NOT READY TO LISTEN TO.

not to hammer people with teachings they are not ready to listen to. Instead, He first demonstrated that He desired people's good and won their confidence by ministering to their needs. Then He invited them to follow Him.

In the work of teaching and healing, personal effort is more powerful than corporate projects. Kindness, courtesy, and unselfishness are tools the Holy Spirit uses to transform lives (143, 144, 156–159).

With our emphasis on public evangelism and television ministries, have we become more of a talking church (teaching) than a doing church (healing)? Jesus always combined the doing and the preaching type of ministry. What does this chapter imply about doing television or mass book and tract distribution in the absence of personal effort for people in a community? When it comes to engaging the world for Christ, do we do it on our terms or are we willing to engage the world on its terms?

As we do missionary outreach, we need to think about the ethics of missionary outreach. Why do we do it? What is the long-term impact of short-term effort? Can we sometimes do more harm than good in the way we reach out?

While theory in itself may not be practical, there is nothing more practical than a good theory. The right theory leads to right practice. For example, we become like the God we worship.

QUOTABLE QUOTES

"Is not faith in the Bible as effectually destroyed by the higher criticism and speculation of today as it was by tradition and rabbinism in the days of Christ? Have not greed and ambition and love of pleasure as strong a hold on men's hearts now as they had then? In the professedly Christian world, even in the professed churches of Christ, how few are governed by Christian principles."

"Christ's method alone will give true success in reaching the people. The Saviour mingled with men as one who desired their good. He showed His sympathy for them, ministered to their needs, and won their confidence. Then He bade them, 'Follow Me.' "

"There is need of coming close to the people by personal effort. If less time were given to sermonizing, and more time were spent in personal ministry, greater results would be seen. . . . We are to weep with those that weep, and rejoice with those that rejoice. Accompanied by the power of persuasion, the power of prayer, the power of the love of God, this work will not, cannot, be without fruit."

"Everywhere there is a tendency to substitute the work of organizations for individual effort. Human wisdom tends to consolidation, to centralization, to the building up of great churches and institutions. Multitudes leave to institutions and organizations the work of benevolence; they excuse themselves from contact with the world, and their hearts grow cold. They become self-absorbed and unimpressible. Love for God and man dies out of the soul."

"Educated workers who are consecrated to God can do service in a greater variety of ways and can accomplish more extensive work than can those who are uneducated. Their discipline of mind places them on vantage ground."

"Men deficient in school education, lowly in social position, have, through the grace of Christ, sometimes been wonderfully successful in winning souls for Him. The secret of their success was their confidence in God."

"It is of little use to try to reform others by attacking what we may regard as wrong habits. Such effort often results in more harm than good."

"Of all people in the world, reformers should be the most unselfish, the most kind, the most courteous. . . . The worker who manifests a lack of courtesy, who shows impatience at the ignorance on waywardness of others, who speaks hastily or acts thoughtlessly, may close the door to hearts so that he can never reach them."

"There is no limit to the usefulness of one who, putting self aside, makes room for the working of the Holy Spirit upon his heart and lives a life wholly consecrated to God. All who consecrate body, soul, and spirit to His service will be constantly receiving a new endowment of physical, mental, and spiritual power. The inexhaustible supplies of heaven are at their command."

@TWEETS_OF_HEALING

In the wrk of the #gospel, teaching & healing r nvr 2 b separated.

In the professedly #Christian world, few r governed by #Christian principles.

@Christ's method alone will give true #success in reaching the ppl.

If less time were given 2 sermonizing & more time were spent in #personalministry, gr8er results would b seen.

Many hve no #faith in @God & hve lost confidence in man. bt they appreciate acts of sympathy & helpfulness.

Thr is a tendency 2 substitute the wrk of organizations 4 #individual effort.

#Truth that is not lived, that is not imparted, loses its life-giving #power.

None need w8 until called 2 some distant field b4 beginning 2 help others. Doors of #service r open everywhere.

Of all ppl in the world, #reformers should b the most #unselfish, the most #kind, the most #courteous.

Naturally we r #selfcentered & #opinionated.

#Wordsofkindness r as welcome as the smile of #angels.

In our #outreach, tlking must b accompanied by doing or it will fall on deaf ears.

Thr is nothng more #practical than a good #theory.

We need 2 think more abt the #ethics of missionary #outreach.

DISCUSSION QUESTIONS

1. In this chapter, we are encouraged to point the sick and suffering to Jesus. But this was written at a time when American culture was truly

Christian. How would Ellen White encourage us to apply this principle in today's world?

2. If Ellen White were alive today, would she say that Adventist hospitals and universities, or similar Adventist institutions, are too big in the context of today's world? Or are things simply different today than in her day?
3. In this chapter, we are encouraged to move from the felt needs of patients to the gospel. How do you actually do that in practice?
4. When it comes to engaging the world for Christ, do we do it on our terms or are we willing to engage the world on its terms?

HELPING THE TEMPTED

CH. 10, PP. 161-169

SUMMARY

Grace is a core feature of God's nature, and is exercised toward undeserving human beings. The more we treat others the way God treats us, the more we can help the tempted and the erring.

THOUGHTS

God does not treat us as we deserve. Every human being is the object of His loving interest. Christ's example in these things is the standard of our service for the tempted and the erring. We are to manifest the same tenderness toward others that He has manifested toward us.

In dealing with the erring, many feel it is important to represent the justice of God. But this fails on two counts. (1) It fails to represent His tenderness and great love. (2) People make positive changes when they are approached with love and grace, they tend to rebel when approached with severity and criticism. The only class of people that Christ treated with severity and criticism was the class that stood apart in their self-esteem and looked down on others (Pharisees).

Methodism at the time had a very similar focus on the love of God. The Methodist idea of perfection was not absolute, but meant living a life of love in response to God's love. But while Ellen White can use Methodist language, she never talks about the "second blessing" of perfection that Wesley spoke about.

Why would God treat Pharisees differently? Don't they need grace and nurture as much as anyone else? We should remember that even when rebuking people Jesus had "tears in His voice."

Jesus treated everyone with respect, even those who had fallen the lowest in depravity, enmity, and impurity. He never acted shocked or offended. He met each person with tenderness and encouragement. It is humiliating to have our mistakes pointed out, so we should not make the experience more bitter by needless censure. Reproach repels, gentleness attracts. We destroy those we seek to help when we show the least amount of disrespect, indifference, or distrust.

How to reconcile the above paragraph with the *Testimonies,* which often pointed out sins in a way that could be experienced as humiliating? It is interesting that Methodists had spiritual clubs in which it was a major focus to point out flaws in the character of others in order to encourage self-improvement. Coming out of that background, Ellen White would not have seen a contradiction between the graceful words of this chapter and the need at times to point out flaws in others. But such rebuke must occur in the context of loving relationship.

Ellen White's writings are much more grace oriented after 1888. But that doesn't mean she changed her view, rather her emphasis shifted from a more eschatological (end-time) approach (the bulk of *The Great Controversy* was written in the pre-1888 period) to a more soteriological one (salvation). Interestingly, the New Testament uses eschatological language to talk about salvation.

A major reason people struggle with Ellen White is that people are prone to taking the "wrong medicine." Pharisees tend to gravitate toward the statements that point out flaws and become more discouraged. Grace-oriented people gravitate to the grace-filled statements and don't always allow themselves to be confronted by obedience.

QUOTABLE QUOTES

"Grace is an attribute of God exercised toward undeserving human beings. We did not seek for it, but it was sent in search of us. God rejoices to bestow His grace upon us, not because we are worthy, but because we are so utterly unworthy. Our only claim to His mercy is our great need."

"By the mystery and glory of the cross we are to discern His estimate of the value of the soul. When we do this, we shall feel that human beings,

JESUS TREATED EVERYONE WITH RESPECT, EVEN THOSE WHO HAD FALLEN THE LOWEST IN DEPRAVITY, ENMITY AND IMPURITY.

however degraded, have cost too much to be treated with coldness or contempt."

"The inhumanity of man toward man is our greatest sin. Many think that they are representing the justice of God while they wholly fail of representing His tenderness and His great love."

"The love of Christ, manifested in word and act, will win its way to the soul, when the reiteration of precept or argument would accomplish nothing."

"Christ honored man with His confidence and thus placed him on his honor. Even those who had fallen the lowest He treated with respect. It was a continual pain to Christ to be brought into contact with enmity, depravity, and impurity; but never did He utter one expression to show that His sensibilities were shocked or His refined tastes offended. Whatever the evil habits, the strong prejudices, or the overbearing passions of human beings, He met them all with pitying tenderness. As we partake of His Spirit, we shall regard all men as brethren, with similar temptations and trials, often falling and struggling to rise again, battling with discouragements and difficulties, craving sympathy and help. Then we shall meet them in such a way as not to discourage or repel them, but to awaken hope in their hearts."

"Many a poor soul is misunderstood, unappreciated, full of distress and agony. . . . Oh, let no word be spoken to cause deeper pain!"

@TWEETS_OF_HEALING

Our only claim 2 @God's mercy is our gr8 need.

At the #cross we discern the true value of the #soul.

The inhumanity of #man toward man is our gr8est sin.

The #love of @Christ wins its way into the #soul, when the recital of arguments would accomplish nothng.

@Christ honored man wt His #confidence & thus placed him on his #honor.

Even those who had #fallen the lowest @Jesus treated wt #respect.

As we partake of His #Spirit, we shall regard all others as #brothers & #sisters.

Reproach repels, #gentleness attracts.

Many r misunderstood, unappreciated & full of #distress & #agony. Let no wrd b spoken 2 cause deeper #pain!

DISCUSSION QUESTIONS

1. According to this chapter, everyone is to be treated with respect, gentleness, and encouragement. How would you reconcile this counsel with the *Testimonies,* where sins are pointed out in a fairly blunt way?
2. What steps can one take to ensure that he or she will read the counsel of Ellen White in a balanced way?

WORKING FOR THE INTEMPERATE

CH. 11, PP. 171–182

SUMMARY

This chapter comes as close as anywhere in the book to describing what we would call addictions. The key in working with the intemperate is to arouse in them the necessity of making an effort for themselves. They are all too ready to let others do the work for them, which will be in vain.

THOUGHTS

We need to be careful in using this chapter today. The language of some parts might play differently today than the author intended. Ellen White modified her language when circumstances changed (for example, there is a lot of war language in the chapter, reflecting the Civil War context of her original health vision). There is also an American "can-do" tone to the chapter. But today, it may be best to read this chapter as the language of aspiration rather than obligation. To the addicted, the language of obligation often discourages and makes things worse. A sobering reality is that while Christians are more likely to point people to Jesus as the answer to addictions, they also suffer a disproportionate share of addictive behaviors compared to the secular mainstream (according to statistical surveys).

A general observation from the last several chapters: it may be surprising to many readers how much of an emphasis on grace there is in nearly every chapter of *The Ministry of Healing.*

According to this chapter, avoiding addictive behavior is rooted in temperance. When people are young they tend to develop intemperate habits that when indulged lead to a form of slavery. When dealing with the intemperate we are not dealing with sane people, it is as if they are under the power of a demon. Keep in mind that temperance back then did not mean moderation, it was more like abstinence in our terms.

When dealing with addictions today, the most helpful thing is grace. In the context of grace, addicts may be able to make an effort for themselves.

With the intemperate, it is critical to speak no word of censure or reproach because they are usually reproaching themselves. Rather, speak words that encourage faith and positive traits of character. One must stay especially close to this class, and they are likely to fall over and over again. Their will power has been weakened.

The key is to arouse in them the necessity of making an effort for themselves. All efforts from outside will be in vain unless they take part in the battle. Everything depends on the right action of the will. There is a sense in which this is impossible for the addicted, yet if they will choose to serve God, He will work in them to re-orient the whole nature over time. While this paragraph could be misused, it is supported in principle by recent research in brain plasticity (the brain's ability to change in response to behavior).

When addicted, it is even more critical to live in obedience to all the principles of health. These will reduce the craving for unnatural stimulants. The intemperate also should be provided employment. None who are able to labor should be taught to expect food and clothing and shelter free of cost. For their sake as well as others, a way must be found where they can provide an equivalent for what they receive. The best kind of work for them is work that helps others in some way.

On pages 180–182 are found some very strong statements about perfect obedience that have struck many as discouraging and impossible to fulfill (see the last quote). These need to be read in light of two things. First, they cannot be understood apart from the grace of God that both accepts the erring (whole previous chapters make that point) and can work in us what we could not do on our own. Second, Ellen White's definition of perfection is a practical one, a doable one. It means "be all that you can be," to live in complete willingness to please God. Why would a Christian want to live any other way?

In our work with addictions today, we have moved from a moral model to an illness model. Current research, however, shows the issue is more complex than simply one or the other. It may be more of a blend between biology and personal choices.

QUOTABLE QUOTES

"You must hold fast to those whom you are trying to help, else victory will never be yours. They will be continually tempted to evil. Again and again they will be almost overcome by the craving for strong drink; again and again they may fall; but do not, because of this, cease your efforts."

"The victims of evil habit must be aroused to the necessity of making an effort for themselves. Others may put forth the most earnest endeavor to uplift them, the grace of God may be freely offered, Christ may entreat, His angels may minister; but all will be in vain unless they themselves are roused to fight the battle in their own behalf."

"Those who put their trust in Christ are not to be enslaved by any hereditary or cultivated habit or tendency. Instead of being held in bondage to the lower nature, they are to rule every appetite and passion. God has not left us to battle with evil in our own finite strength. Whatever may be our inherited or cultivated tendencies to wrong, we can overcome through the power that He is ready to impart."

"The tempted one needs to understand the true force of the will. This is the governing power in the nature of man—the power of decision, of choice. Everything depends on the right action of the will. Desires for goodness and purity are right, so far as they go; but if we stop here, they avail nothing."

"When light flashes into the soul, some who appeared to be most fully given to sin will become successful workers for just such sinners as they themselves once were. . . . They see where their own weakness lies, they realize the depravity of their nature. They know the strength of sin, the power of evil habit. They realize their inability to overcome without the help of Christ. . . . These can help others."

"Christ lived a life of perfect obedience to God's law, and in this He set an example for every human being. The life that He lived in this world we are to live through His power and under His instruction. . . . Nothing less than perfect obedience can meet the standard of God's requirement. He has not left His requirements indefinite. He has enjoined nothing that is not necessary in order to bring man into harmony with Him. We are to point sinners to His ideal of character and to lead them to Christ, by whose grace only can this ideal be reached."

@TWEETS_OF_HEALING

The #addicted must b aroused 2 the necessity of making an effort for themselves.

Those who put their #trust in @Christ r not 2 b #enslaved by any hereditary or cultivated #habit or tendency.

Everything depends on the right action of the #will.

Through the right #exercise of the #will, an entire chng may b made in the #life, we ally ourselves wt #divine pwr.

None who r able 2 labor should b taught 2 expect food & clothing & shelter #freeofcost.

Nothng less than #perfectobedience cn meet the standard of @God's requirement.

#Humanity, combined wt #divinity, does not commit #sin.

Those whom @Christ has #forgiven most will #love #Him most.

DISCUSSION QUESTIONS

1. To addicts the language of obligation often leads to failure. So how do we reconcile the counsel of this chapter with our experience of addictive behavior in today's world?
2. How do you balance the language of this chapter with the gracious, forgiving and self-sacrificing character of God portrayed in the early chapters of the book?

HELP FOR THE UNEMPLOYED AND THE HOMELESS

CH. 12, PP. 182-200

SUMMARY

The ultimate solution to unemployment and homelessness will not be found in education or government programs, but in implementing God's plan for Israel; providing the means and the incentive for a useful, industrious and self-supporting life.

THOUGHTS

A caveat to the theme of this chapter is the next, "The Helpless Poor." There, Ellen White recognizes that there are some who are unable to support themselves, no matter how much incentive one might provide. These will always need charity or a safety net of some sort.

At the time *The Ministry of Healing* was written, New York City was the size of San Bernardino, California, or Lincoln, Nebraska. That raises the question of the degree to which the remedy of this chapter could be implemented in the context of the megalopolis, which is where an increasing percentage of the world's population lives (vast distances from city center to true country living). Could one implement God's plan for Israel in Cairo or Dacca or even New York City today in a way that would make a discernable difference to the urban context? How would one do that?

As Ellen White describes it, God's plan for Israel was that every family would have a home on the land, with sufficient ground for tilling. This is what today we call subsistence farming. But in an age of factory farms (it takes almost 5,000 acres in many places to break even), farm subsidies and trade wars, could people in the West survive on subsistence farming anymore? In the original context of this chapter, the counsel made a lot of sense. Have circumstances changed so much that Ellen White would rewrite the chapter drastically today? This is not a statement of doubt, rather of following through on her own principle of "circumstances alter cases." We need to recognize that these are complex issues and we need the Holy Spirit's guidance to rightly apply Ellen White's counsel today.

One thing to keep in mind while reading this chapter is that the nineteenth century had a somewhat romanticized view of nature and her comments fit within that context. She also shares a somewhat Victorian attitude toward the problems of the city, and most cities were quite unattractive in those days. The Victorians tended to read the Pentateuch in light of their own city problems and Ellen White did much the same. On the other hand, her comments track very well with many current environmentalists, who are calling for a decentralization of land ownership. There is a trend in her argument that is being picked up more and more today. A related trend is a proliferation of urban rooftop gardens, even with bee colonies. In some third world countries, suicide rates are high among farmers because centralization of land ownership makes it impossible for small farmers to take care of their families.

The principle of the jubilee is an interesting one. Some economists have suggested that it would eliminate inflation, as the value of land would be constantly declining—measured in the number of years of crops that remained before the land would revert to the original owner. Again, this principle is grounded in the role of subsistence farming in the ancient economy.

Ellen White summarizes God's plan for Israel as follows: ownership of tillable land, industrial training (how to work with one's hands), provision for the poor (gleaning), liberality in giving, and sound and just business principles. This plan may not be realistic in all cases today (think Hong Kong). With regard to teeming urban slums, however, one could perhaps imagine a rotation system where the poorest of the poor could experience the benefits of the above and then bring those principles back to the city and work for their neighbors and friends.

The best kind of charity work helps people to help themselves. We harm the poor when our well-intentioned efforts teach them to be dependent. As a rule, it takes training to develop habits of industry, perseverance, economy, and self-denial.

QUOTABLE QUOTES

"Within the vast boundaries of nature there is still room for the suffering and needy to find a home. Within her bosom there are resources sufficient to provide them with food. Hidden in the depths of the earth are blessings for all who have courage and will and perseverance to gather her treasures."

"Many look upon labor as drudgery, and they try to obtain a livelihood by scheming rather than by honest toil. This desire to get a living without work opens the door to wretchedness and vice and crime almost without limit."

"We may give to the poor, and harm them, by teaching them to be dependent. Such giving encourages selfishness and helplessness. Often it leads to idleness, extravagance, and intemperance. . . . The world owes no man a living who is able to work and gain a living for himself."

"Real charity helps men to help themselves. If one comes to our door and asks for food, we should not turn him away hungry; his poverty may be the result of misfortune. But true beneficence means more than mere gifts. It means a genuine interest in the welfare of others. We should seek to understand the needs of the poor and distressed, and to give them the help that will benefit them most. To give thought and time and personal effort costs far more than merely to give money. But it is the truest charity."

"Simplicity, self-denial, economy, lessons so essential for the poor to learn, often seem to them difficult and unwelcome. The example and spirit of the world is constantly exciting and fostering pride, love of display, self-indulgence, prodigality, and idleness. These evils bring thousands to penury and prevent thousands more from rising out of degradation and wretchedness. Christians are to encourage the poor to resist these influences."

"Jesus sought to correct the world's false standard of judging the value of men. He took His position with the poor, that He might lift from poverty the stigma that the world had attached to it."

@TWEETS_OF_HEALING

Wtin the vast boundaries of #nature thr is still room for the #suffering & #needy 2 find a #home.

Giving 2 the #poor is harmful if it teaches them 2 b dependent.

Real #charity helps ppl help themselves.

To give thought & time & personal #effort costs far more than merely 2 give #money, bt it's the truest #charity.

#Bible #religion nvr makes ppl idlers.

#Kindness will accomplish more than #censure.

@Jesus sought 2 correct the world's false standard of judging the #value of #men. He took His position wt the #poor.

#Life's best things—simplicity, honesty, truthfulness, purity, integrity—cannot b bought or sold.

He who owns the #world is #rich in resources & will #bless every1 who is seeking 2 #blessothers.

DISCUSSION QUESTIONS

1. At the time *The Ministry of Healing* was written, New York City was the size of San Bernardino, California, or Lincoln, Nebraska. To what degree can the solutions offered in this chapter be applied in the context of the megalopolis? Can one implement God's plan for Israel in Cairo or Dacca in a way that would make a discernable difference to the urban context? How would one start?
2. In an age when it takes as much as 5,000 acres for a farmer to break even, are the counsels in this chapter doable? Would Ellen White drastically rewrite the chapter if she lived today?

THE HELPLESS POOR

CH. 13, PP. 201-208

SUMMARY

When one has done everything possible to help the poor help themselves, there will still remain some who cannot help themselves; the widow and fatherless, the aged, the helpless, and the sick. These should not be neglected.

THOUGHTS

These are the ones who need a "safety net." The problem is, the same programs that are life-enhancing and life-saving for the helpless poor can do more harm than good for those who could help themselves. How can one help the helpless poor without damaging those who aren't helpless?

Circumstances have changed, but many of the same issues remain today, orphans, single-mothers, the aged. The major plan for orphans today is foster care and these programs have too-often failed; they offer children no sense of permanent family and then turn them loose at age eighteen. Too often they end up in trouble with the law. One recent solution: "residential academies," housing teens in groups with proper oversight and counseling. In Ellen White's day, people often put unwanted children on trains heading west, hoping that at some stop a family would pick them up and take care of them.

Ministry to the helpless poor should begin with "the household of faith."

Single mothers are a special case. They are not helpless, yet their responsibilities are so overwhelming many times that they are forced to choose between earning money and the proper upbringing of their children. Help with child care and moral training can be a major support.

Where possible, people should be allowed to "age in place," among friends and familiar associations, worshiping among those they have known and loved. Multi-generational churches can be a great blessing. The young bring energy and sunshine to the aged and the aged bring wisdom and experience to the young. This underlines that retirement at your "dream location" may not turn out well if you leave your support system and community behind.

Where orphanages are required, they should be modeled as closely as possible upon the Christian home.

Given the world's great needs in regard to the helpless poor, everyone, regardless of financial circumstances, should practice economy so they can help others and not make them envious.

EVERYONE, REGARDLESS OF FINANCIAL CIRCUMSTANCES, SHOULD PRACTICE ECONOMY SO THEY CAN HELP OTHERS AND NOT MAKE THEM ENVIOUS.

The anthropology behind this chapter is that human value is not based on production, but on the reality that everyone is a soul for whom Christ died. All the helpless are worthy of support because their value was set at the Cross.

In today's world, we have become more aware that the system defines poverty more than the person. Many people today have lost jobs and homes without any fault of their own, defeated by a system. Do we realize how much place and parentage have so much to do with what we have and who we are? This chapter doesn't address such systemic issues, but that doesn't mean Ellen White would not have addressed them were she writing today. For example, while she regretted that churches did not do more for the former slaves in the south, she supported the government's efforts at Reconstruction and chastised the government when it cut back on that support. Additionally, the main purpose of *The Ministry of Healing* was mission. She is not addressing social issues, but teaching health practitioners how to reach different classes of people with the gospel. Next chapter? Dealing with the rich.

QUOTABLE QUOTES

"Many who have no children of their own could do a good work in caring for the children of others. Instead of giving attention to pets, lavishing affection upon dumb animals, let them give their attention to little children, whose characters they may fashion after the divine similitude. Place your love upon the homeless members of the human family."

"So far as possible let those whose whitening heads and failing steps show that they are drawing near to the grave remain among friends and familiar associations. Let them worship among those whom they have known and loved. Let them be cared for by loving and tender hands."

"Many despise economy, confounding it with stinginess and narrowness. But. . . . without economy, there can be no true liberality. We are to save, that we may give."

"How much means is expended for things that are mere idols, things that engross thought and time and strength which should be put to a higher use! How much money is wasted on expensive houses and furniture, on selfish pleasures, luxurious and unwholesome food, hurtful indulgences! How much is squandered on gifts that benefit no one! For things that are needless, often harmful, professed Christians are today spending more, many times more, than they spend in seeking to rescue souls from the tempter."

"It is wrong to waste our time, wrong to waste our thoughts. We lose every moment that we devote to self-seeking. If every moment were valued and rightly employed, we should have time for everything that we need to do for ourselves or for the world. In the expenditure of money, in the use of time, strength, opportunities, let every Christian look to God for guidance."

@TWEETS_OF_HEALING

#Ministry 2 the helpless #poor should begin wt "the household of #faith."

#Children develop best in the #loving atmosphere of a @Christian #home.

Many who hve no #children of their own cld do a #good wrk in caring for the #children of #others.

Wtout economy, thr cn b no true liberality. We r 2 #save, that we may #give.

How much #money is squandered on #gifts that benefit no one!

It is wrong 2 waste our #time, wrong 2 waste our thoughts. We lose every #moment that we devote 2 self-seeking.

If every #moment were #valued & rightly employed, we would hve #time for everything that we need 2 do.

DISCUSSION QUESTIONS

1. How can one help the helpless poor without damaging the poor who are not helpless?
2. Why do you think Ellen White doesn't address the systemic basis of poverty, the way place and parentage affect what we have and who we are?

MINISTRY TO THE RICH

CH. 14, PP. 209-216

SUMMARY

Special efforts are to be made to reach out to the rich, who face special challenges in coming to the gospel; such as business entanglements and associations, overwhelming responsibilities, the glitter of earthly glory, lack of self-control, and the vanity of material things.

THOUGHTS

In this chapter, Ellen White addresses what you do with your money rather than how you got it (as in the book of James). The Wessels family became extremely wealthy, but she never speaks ill of them and how they got their wealth, perhaps because they were so generous with it. Today we are more aware that there are institutions and systems that keep people from flourishing. She doesn't address such institutional disparities. But we don't have to limit our concerns only to the things she addresses.

The kinds of things that Ellen White identifies as unique challenges that face the wealthy are now faced by nearly everyone in the West through the media and the Internet. The lives of even the poorest today are way more complicated than a century ago, filled with responsibilities, temptations to abandon self-control, and to envy the rich and famous, thereby focusing on attention from others and the vanity of material things. But the rich today still face one unique challenge. The poor can always dream that riches will solve their problems, the rich know that riches don't.

Because of their power and influence in everyday life, the rich and famous do not see the necessity of self-control in all things, thus they are in greater danger of habits that ruin both body and soul. Temperance work built on principle is needed with them. They need to understand how harmful indulgences lessen the physical, mental, and moral powers they have received in abundance. They can do a lot of good with the money that they spend on things that do them harm.

The rich have the greatest capacity to benefit the needy, yet, absorbed in worldly treasure, they are often the least aware of the claims of God and the needs of others. They use their wealth to glorify themselves rather than change the world in a positive way.

Those best fitted to work for the higher classes should study how to reach these people, how to awaken them to the needs of their soul for what the gospel offers. They are best won, not by elaborate arguments and expensive dress, but by a consistent, unselfish, and winsome simplicity.

Wealthy people, when converted to Christ, are well fitted to work for others of their class.

It is interesting to compare Ellen White's description of Paul in Athens in *The Acts of the Apostles* and *The Ministry of Healing.* Her view of Paul's success or lack of it in Athens is more positive in the former than the latter.

One of the difficult things about reaching the rich is that it is hard for them to trust anyone. Most people who approach them have ulterior motives. The rich don't appreciate people trying to impress them or be like them. "Meeting the rich where they are" doesn't require big homes or flashy cars. The best way to work for the rich is to set an example of concern for the poor.

In the healing professions, how much money can one make and still have "acquired wealth honestly"? What does it mean today to gain riches honestly when systems so often favor one class over another?

QUOTABLE QUOTES

"Few among [the rich] go to church; for they feel that they receive little benefit. The teaching they hear does not touch the heart. Shall we make no personal appeal to them?"

"The cup most difficult to carry is not the cup that is empty, but the cup that is full to the brim. It is this that needs to be most carefully balanced.

WEALTHY PEOPLE, WHEN CONVERTED TO CHRIST, ARE WELL FITTED TO WORK FOR OTHERS OF THEIR CLASS.

Affliction and adversity bring disappointment and sorrow; but it is prosperity that is most dangerous to spiritual life."

"Often prayer is solicited for those who are suffering from illness or adversity; but our prayers are most needed by the men entrusted with prosperity and influence."

"The Bible condemns no man for being rich, if he has acquired his riches honestly. Not money, but the love of money, is the root of all evil."

"Some are especially fitted to work for the higher classes. These should seek wisdom from God to know how to reach these persons, to have not merely a casual acquaintance with them, but by personal effort and living faith to awaken them to the needs of the soul, to lead them to a knowledge of the truth as it is in Jesus."

"The way of worldly policy is not God's way of reaching the higher classes. That which will reach them effectually is a consistent, unselfish presentation of the gospel of Christ."

"In the work for this class many discouragements will be presented, many heartsickening revelations will be made. But all things are possible with God."

"When it is made plain that the Lord expects them as His representatives to relieve suffering humanity, many will respond and will give of their means and their sympathies for the benefit of the poor. As their minds are thus drawn away from their own selfish interests, many will surrender themselves to Christ."

@TWEETS_OF_HEALING

The #poor cn always #dream that riches will solve their problems, the #rich know that riches don't.

Riches & worldly #honor cn not satisfy the #soul.

Few among the #rich go 2 #church; for they feel that they receive little benefit.

The cup most difficult 2 carry is not the #cup that is #empty, bt the cup that is full 2 the #brim.

It is not #money, bt the #love of money, that is the root of all #evil.

It is by no casual #touch or acquaintance that the #wealthy cn b drawn 2 @Christ.

All things r possible wt @God.

DISCUSSION QUESTIONS

1. In the healing professions, how much can one make and still have "acquired wealth honestly"? What does it mean today to gain riches honestly when systems so often favor one class over another?
2. While this chapter is about ministry to the rich, many of the challenges that the rich faced in Ellen White's day sound similar to what everyone in the West faces through the media and the Internet. What elements in this chapter speak with particular cogency to our contemporary situation?

IN THE SICKROOM

CH. 15, PP. 219-224

SUMMARY

This chapter addresses caregivers, nurses in particular. Where disease is involved, both caregivers and patients require extra attention to the laws of health.

THOUGHTS

In many ways, this chapter addresses issues of what we would today call public health: good air, clean water and surroundings, the right kind of and balance in diet. Sanitation in the sickroom is still a critical issue today since many illnesses and deaths arise from the hospital environment and things like errors in filling prescriptions. Health care requires great care concerning treatment and the environment in which the treatment is given.

The first part of the chapter addresses caregivers, such as nurses. Attending to the sick involves some peril to oneself. So principles of healthful living are all the more important for active caregivers. The better their health, the better they can handle the strain. So they need to give special attention to diet, cleanliness, fresh air, and exercise. Where a patient needs around the clock care, a rotation of caregivers is advised, so that each can remain rested and exercised. With proper precautions, such as ventilation and cleanliness, caregivers need not contract the patient's illness.

The second part of the chapter addresses the care of the sick in practical terms. The sickroom needs to be well ventilated, yet an even temperature should be maintained as far as possible. The patient's diet should be healthy, but care should be given that they not eat too much or too little. The one undernourishes the system at a time it needs help, the other overtaxes digestive organs at a time when they are weakened.

For the patient's sake, caregivers should be cheerful and calm. Excitement, hurry, and confusion should be avoided. For those who are extremely sick, visitation should be discouraged.

In as kind and tender a manner as possible, caregivers are to teach the laws of health and the consequences of wrong habits. Where possible, they should be introduced to Christ as a Friend who will be close to them at this time. Physical and spiritual care go hand in hand.

The advice given in this chapter is a fine line in patient care between the calmness, tenderness, and encouragement the caregiver needs to express and education or "confrontation" regarding wrong habits. It is not clear from the chapter exactly how this balance is to be maintained in practical terms, but at the personal level much expression of acceptance and approval should precede confrontation. With regard to public health today, a certain corporate confrontation occurs when laws restrict smoking and ensure clean air and water, even if some citizens feel coerced in the process.

An unspoken implication of this chapter is that we should not expect miracles in the sickroom as a regular matter. Prayer is "soothing" to the patients and a sense of God's presence aids healing, but most of the advice here concerns not divine miracles, but things human beings can do to aid in the healing process. Early in Ellen White's experience, she saw the negative outcomes of choosing prayer in place of a physician's care. Her counsel has always been to combine prayer with every possible human means of healing at our disposal.

QUOTABLE QUOTES

"Those who minister to the sick should understand the importance of careful attention to the laws of health. Nowhere is obedience to these laws more important than in the sickroom. Nowhere does so much depend upon faithfulness in little things on the part of the attendants. In cases of serious illness, a little neglect, a slight inattention to a patient's special needs or dangers, the manifestation of fear, excitement, or petulance, even a lack of sympathy, may turn the scale that is balancing life and death,

PHYSICAL AND SPIRITUAL CARE GO HAND IN HAND.

and cause to go down to the grave a patient who otherwise might have recovered."

"It is misdirected kindness, a false idea of courtesy, that leads to much visiting of the sick. Those who are very ill should not have visitors. The excitement connected with receiving callers wearies the patient at a time when he is in the greatest need of quiet, undisturbed rest. To a convalescent or a patient suffering from chronic disease, it is often a pleasure and a benefit to know that he is kindly remembered; but this assurance conveyed by a message of sympathy or by some little gift will often serve a better purpose than a personal visit, and without danger of harm."

"(Nurses) need ever to remember that in the discharge of their daily duties they are serving the Lord Christ."

"The sick need to have wise words spoken to them. . . . The atmosphere surrounding the soul of the one giving treatment should be pure and fragrant. Physicians and nurses are to cherish the principles of Christ. In their lives His virtues are to be seen. Then, by what they do and say, they will draw the sick to the Saviour."

"In the kindest and tenderest manner nurses are to teach that he who would be healed must cease to transgress the law of God. He must cease to choose a life of sin."

@TWEETS_OF_HEALING

Nowhere is #obedience 2 the laws of #health more important than in the #sickroom.

The better their #health, the better #caregivers cn endure the strain of attending 2 the #sick.

Those who care for the #sick should give special attention 2 diet, cleanliness, fresh air & #exercise.

Those who r very #ill should not hve visitors.

#Caregivers need ever 2 remember that they r really #serving @Jesus.

#Caregivers should b ever ready 2 blend #spiritualhealing wt #physicalhealing.

He or she who would b #healed must cease 2 transgress the #law of @God.

DISCUSSION QUESTIONS

Read: *"Care should be taken so to prepare and serve the food that it will be palatable, but wise judgment should be used in adapting it to the needs of the patient, both in quantity and quality."*

1. Should Adventist hospitals offer meat to those patients who so desire or not? Why?

Read: *"In the kindest and tenderest manner nurses are to teach that he who would be healed must cease to transgress the law of God. He must cease to choose a life of sin."* (Ellen G. White is talking in a nineteenth-century context, where everybody is considered a Christian).

2. How do you do that in the twenty-first century, when many people do not profess faith? How do you blend "spiritual" and "physical" healing in the Adventist health ministries and health institutions context?

PRAYER FOR THE SICK

CH. 16, PP. 225–233

SUMMARY

The main thesis of this chapter seems to be that God is just as willing to restore the sick to health now as He was in biblical times. His disciples today are to be as active in prayer for the sick as the disciples of old were.

THOUGHTS

When those who attend the sick live in the presence of God, the sick come to the conviction that God is with them in a healing presence, and this conviction will do much to heal both soul and body.

When it comes to praying for the sick it is important to consider the role of both repentance and obedience. Where sickness has been caused by disregard for nature's laws of health, miraculous healing might only confirm someone in their destructive indulgences. So in praying for the sick, it is important to encourage repentance and a willingness to do that which fosters health in the future. We should not expect from God a miracle that will encourage sin.

People need to be encouraged to trust in God. To be anxious about oneself tends toward weakness and disease. In an atmosphere of trust and peace there is healing power. While we should pray according to God's will, we need to trust that God's will is the best thing for us. When we trust in God, we can be at peace about the outcome. God knows the end from the beginning, including the outcome that would occur if healing should take place. So if people are not healed when we pray for healing, we should not conclude that they or we did not have faith.

WE SHOULD NOT EXPECT FROM GOD A MIRACLE THAT WILL ENCOURAGE SIN.

There is a fine line between encouraging the exercise of faith in prayer regardless of former indiscretions and emphasizing the obligation to a change of life and habits, which could be discouraging to some.

While Ellen White encourages prayer for the sick, we need to be honest that scientific attempts to test the power of prayer have offered mixed results. (See *The American Heart Journal* 151, no. 4 [April 2006]: 934–942, which found no benefit to intercessory prayer, and *The Southern Medical Journal* 81, no. 7 [July 1988]: 826–829, or *Archives of Internal Medicine* 163, no. 12 [June 2003]: 1405–1408, which did.) Ellen White herself seems to begin this chapter with a strong statement on the power of prayer and then move to a more rational approach to disease by the end of the chapter. This chapter flow seems to mirror the flow of her life as well. Her earliest ministry was strong on miracles and she was reluctant to go to doctors. Later she was much more positive about health practices and scientific health care. Her great health vision of 1863, of course, must have played a major role in that shift.

One point that is crucial about all these studies: the overwhelming majority of people in our day who pray don't get miraculous healings. It happens at times but it is not the norm. And it was not the norm during most eras described in the Bible. Biblical miracles are largely clustered around the Exodus, the time of Elijah and Elisha, and the time of Jesus and His disciples. The statement in *Testimonies for the Church,* volume 1, page 561 is instructive: "Let no one obtain the idea that the Institute is the place for them to come to be raised up by the prayer of faith. That is the place to find relief from disease by treatment and right habits of living, and to learn how to avoid sickness. But if there is one place under the heavens more than another where soothing, sympathizing prayer should be offered by men and women of devotion and faith it is at such an institute. Those who treat the sick should move forward in their important work with strong reliance upon God for His blessing to attend the means which He has graciously provided, and to which He has in mercy called our attention as a people, such as pure air, cleanliness, healthful diet, proper periods of labor and repose, and the use of water."

A colleague suggested a pattern in prayer that is helpful. Prayer begins with frank expressions to God of the desire of our hearts (healing, etc.), but the same prayer can and should end with "Thy will be done." The latter is not truly expressed until the former has been expressed.

QUOTABLE QUOTES

"When human strength fails, men feel their need of divine help. And never does our merciful God turn from the soul that in sincerity seeks Him for help."

"God is just as willing to restore the sick to health now as when the Holy Spirit spoke these words through the psalmist. And Christ is the same compassionate physician now that He was during His earthly ministry. In Him there is healing balm for every disease, restoring power for every infirmity. His disciples in this time are to pray for the sick as verily as the disciples of old prayed. And recoveries will follow; for 'the prayer of faith shall save the sick.' "

"Many persons bring disease upon themselves by their self-indulgence. They have not lived in accordance with natural law or the principles of strict purity. Others have disregarded the laws of health in their habits of eating and drinking, dressing, or working. Often some form of vice is the cause of feebleness of mind or body. Should these persons gain the blessing of health, many of them would continue to pursue the same course of heedless transgression of God's natural and spiritual laws, reasoning that if God heals them in answer to prayer, they are at liberty to continue their unhealthful practices and to indulge perverted appetite without restraint. If God were to work a miracle in restoring these persons to health, He would be encouraging sin."

"If any who are seeking health have been guilty of evilspeaking, if they have sowed discord in the home, the neighborhood, or the church, and have stirred up alienation and dissension, if by any wrong practice they have led others into sin, these things should be confessed before God and before those who have been offended."

"When wrongs have been righted, we may present the needs of the sick to the Lord in calm faith, as His Spirit may indicate. He knows each individual by name, and cares for each as if there were not another upon the earth for whom He gave His beloved Son. Because God's love is so great and so unfailing, the sick should be encouraged to trust in Him and be cheerful. To be anxious about themselves tends to cause weakness and disease."

"God is too wise and good to answer our prayers always at just the time and in just the manner we desire. He will do more and better for us than to accomplish all our wishes. And because we can trust His wisdom and love, we should not ask Him to concede to our will, but should seek to enter into and accomplish His purpose."

"Those who seek healing by prayer should not neglect to make use of the remedial agencies within their reach. It is not a denial of faith to use such remedies as God has provided to alleviate pain and to aid nature in her work of restoration."

"When we have prayed for the recovery of the sick, whatever the outcome of the case, let us not lose faith in God. If we are called upon to meet bereavement, let us accept the bitter cup, remembering that a Father's hand holds it to our lips. But should health be restored, it should not be forgotten that the recipient of healing mercy is placed under renewed obligation to the Creator."

@TWEETS_OF_HEALING

Nvr does our merciful @God turn frm the #soul that in sincerity seeks #Him for #help.

@God is as willing now 2 restore the #sick as He was in #biblicaltimes.

We should pray 2 @God as 1 whose purpose is 2 #heal & not destroy.

We should not #expect @God 2 #heal us if we r not willing 2 lay aside #unhealthfulpractices.

@God is too #wise & #good 2 answer our #prayers always at just the time & in just the manner we desire.

Those who #seek #healing by #prayer should not neglect 2 make use of the remedial agencies wtin their reach.

We cn ask @God 2 give us the #prayer He would like us 2 #pray for the #sick.

In an atmosphere of #trust & #peace thr is #healingpower.

DISCUSSION QUESTION

In this chapter, Ellen White is going from the "miraculous" to more rational and practical ways of healing.

See: Matthew 17:20—"He replied, 'Because you have so little faith. Truly I tell you, if you have faith as small as a mustard seed, you can say to this mountain, "Move from here to there" and it will move. Nothing will be impossible for you' " (NIV).

Read: *"Believing that they will be healed in answer to prayer, some fear to do anything that might seem to indicate a lack of faith. . . . Those who seek healing by prayer should not neglect to make use of the remedial agencies within their reach."*

1. How do you relate to the concept of "prayer for the sick"?—Take into account that majority of people in our days do *not* experience "miraculous" healing.

THE USE OF REMEDIES

CH. 17, PP. 234-240

SUMMARY

Disease never comes without a cause. Disease is invited by disregard of the laws of health, either by the individual or through inheritance from the parents. Among the causes of disease are intemperate eating, overwork, inactivity, and excessive mental labor. Among the best remedies for disease are carefulness in diet, the proper use of water, and physical exercise.

THOUGHTS

A very important principle needs to be reiterated here. Ellen White makes many strong, prophetic statements, such as "If we carefully preserve the life force, . . . the result is health." Such statements are best read along the lines of the Proverbs in the Bible. "All other things being equal," the righteous prosper and the wicked suffer. But things are not always equal in this life. Thus some who live impeccable lives in relation to the laws of health die young and others who smoke, drink, and carouse live to be a hundred. There are other factors in play besides obedience or disobedience to the laws of health. "All other things being equal," the health counsels of Ellen White produce better health outcomes, but in a sinful world, things are not always equal. There is always the danger that we will pass judgment on others on the basis of their health outcomes. Such use is a misuse of Ellen White's gift.

There is also the principle of individuality. General principles such as one

THERE IS ALWAYS THE DANGER THAT WE WILL PASS JUDGMENT ON OTHERS ON THE BASIS OF THEIR HEALTH OUTCOMES.

finds in *The Ministry of Healing* work in the majority of cases, but followers of Ellen White's counsel are encouraged to study for themselves and understand what things are beneficial and harmful to them personally; and that is a knowledge that usually does not come from direct inspiration but rather from careful study and observation.

Ellen White herself points to these qualifiers in the very last sentence of the chapter: "*In most cases* if they would eat temperately, and take cheerful, healthful exercise, they would recover health and would save time and money" (italics supplied).

A historical footnote: The concept of a "life force" was common at the time. Some called it the theory of vitalism. Doctors of the time felt that they could project how long someone had left to live by the amount of "vitality" left. This view has largely been abandoned by medicine today, even at Loma Linda, although new iterations of it, such as Hans Selye's "adaptation energy" theory, are still held to have validity.

It needs to be understood that in inspiration God meets people where they are. That means that in communicating truth, God uses the language, cultural concepts, and scientific limitations of the prophet's time to articulate and explain that truth. Thus Ellen White's explanations of health principles may at times express information that cannot be validated scientifically today or may even seem flat-out incorrect. But that is not surprising when one sees how God communicated with the biblical prophets. God does not always disabuse people of their scientific or philosophical oddities, but communicates the truth they need for salvation in terms they can understand. There is a similar process at work in Ellen White's writings.

QUOTABLE QUOTES

"Disease never comes without a cause. The way is prepared, and disease invited, by disregard of the laws of health. Many suffer in consequence of the transgression of their parents. While they are not responsible for what their parents have done, it is nevertheless their duty to ascertain what are and what are not violations of the laws of health. They should avoid the wrong habits of their parents and, by correct living, place themselves in better conditions."

"God has endowed us with a certain amount of vital force. . . . If we carefully preserve the life force, and keep the delicate mechanism of the body in order, the result is health; but if the vital force is too rapidly exhausted, the nervous system borrows power for present use from its resources of strength, and when one organ is injured, all are affected."

"When the abuse of health is carried so far that sickness results, the sufferer can often do for himself what no one else can do for him. The first thing to be done is to ascertain the true character of the sickness and then go to work intelligently to remove the cause."

"Inactivity is a fruitful cause of disease. Exercise quickens and equalizes the circulation of the blood, but in idleness the blood does not circulate freely, and the changes in it, so necessary to life and health, do not take place."

"Ministers, teachers, students, and other brain workers often suffer from illness as the result of severe mental taxation, unrelieved by physical exercise. What these persons need is a more active life. Strictly temperate habits, combined with proper exercise, would ensure both mental and physical vigor, and would give power of endurance to all brain workers."

"When invalids have nothing to occupy their time and attention, their thoughts become centered upon themselves, and they grow morbid and irritable. Many times they dwell upon their bad feelings until they think themselves much worse than they really are and wholly unable to do anything. In all these cases well-directed physical exercise would prove an effective remedial agent. In some cases it is indispensable to the recovery of health."

"Those whose habits are sedentary should, when the weather will permit, exercise in the open air every day, summer or winter. Walking is preferable to riding or driving, for it brings more of the muscles into exercise. The lungs are forced into healthy action, since it is impossible to walk briskly without inflating them. Such exercise would in many cases be better for the health than medicine."

@TWEETS_OF_HEALING

#Disease nvr comes wtout a cause.

@God has endowed every1 wt a certain amount of vital force.

Intemperate #eating is often the cause of #sickness.

When 1 organ is injured, all r affected.

#Inactivity is a fruitful cause of #disease.

When invalids hve nothng 2 occupy their #time & #attention, their thoughts bcome centered upon #themselves.

#Exercise is in many cases bttr 4 #health than #medicine.

DISCUSSION QUESTIONS

Read: *"Disease never comes without a cause."*

1. Do you agree or disagree with the above claim?

Note the paradox: Some who live healthy lives, get sick, and others who may not live so healthy, live long lives. Explain.

1. The reality of sin
2. Inheritance

Read: *"Ministers, teachers, students, and other brain workers—often suffer from illness as the result of severe mental taxation, unrelieved by physical exercise."*

2. Are Adventists affected by lack of physical exercise?

3. What are some of the ways that one can change that as a church or institution that promotes *wholeness*?

MIND **CURE**

CH. 18, PP. 241-258

SUMMARY

The concept of human wholeness implies that there is an intimate relationship between the mind and the body. The condition of the mind has a powerful effect on the health of the body. Grief, anxiety, discontent, and remorse all break down the life forces and invite decay and death. Courage, hope, faith, love, gratitude, and praise promote health and prolong life. Rightly used, mental influence is one of the most effective agencies for combating disease.

THOUGHTS

This is one of the best chapters in all of Ellen White's writings, with profound implications for emotional and psychological health. There are a multitude of quotable quotes in the chapter.

In spite of her strong support for attention to mental health, Ellen White is very negative about one of the major therapies of her day, hypnotism, where one person's mind is brought under the control of another's. She asserts instead that no one is to yield their mind and will to the control of another. Human freedom to think and to do was one of the strongest themes throughout her writing.

Those whose diseases have been caused by the mind are best helped through the exercise of tender sympathy and tact.

Bible principles of "mind cure" include directing patients to Christ, encouraging a positive frame of mind, reciting the promises of the Bible, living in the present (not borrowing problems from an imagined future or wallowing in regret over the past). Above all else, the greatest healing agency is a spirit of gratitude and praise. See the quotes and tweets for many of the details in this powerful chapter. The best portion of all can be found on pages 251–253.

This chapter is about more than just positive thinking. Positive thinking is valuable in current psychological thinking, but people do even better when they are both authentic and positive (there is a dishonest sort of positive thinking). There is a trend in recent mental care to foster more and more positive mental heath, not just deal with disorders. Ellen White seems to put the focus there as well.

QUOTABLE QUOTES

"The relation that exists between the mind and the body is very intimate. When one is affected, the other sympathizes. The condition of the mind affects the health to a far greater degree than many realize. Many of the diseases from which men suffer are the result of mental depression. Grief, anxiety, discontent, remorse, guilt, distrust, all tend to break down the life forces and to invite decay and death.

"Disease is sometimes produced, and is often greatly aggravated, by the imagination. Many are lifelong invalids who might be well if they only thought so. Many imagine that every slight exposure will cause illness, and the evil effect is produced because it is expected. Many die from disease the cause of which is wholly imaginary.

"Courage, hope, faith, sympathy, love, promote health and prolong life. A contented mind, a cheerful spirit, is health to the body and strength to the soul. 'A merry [rejoicing] heart doeth good like a medicine.' Proverbs 17:22."

"We are in a world of suffering. Difficulty, trial, and sorrow await us all along the way to the heavenly home. But there are many who make life's burdens doubly heavy by continually anticipating trouble. . . . Life itself becomes a burden to them. But it need not be thus. It will cost a determined effort to change the current of their thought. But the change can be made. Their happiness, both for this life and for the life to come, depends upon their fixing their minds upon cheerful things. Let them look away from the dark picture, which is imaginary, to the benefits which God has strewn in their pathway."

"It is not wise to look to ourselves and study our emotions. If we do this, the enemy will present difficulties and temptations that weaken faith and destroy courage. Closely to study our emotions and give way to our feelings is to entertain doubt and entangle ourselves in perplexity. We are to look away from self to Jesus. . . . When temptations assail you, when care, perplexity, and darkness seem to surround your soul, look to the place where you last saw the light."

"Nothing tends more to promote health of body and of soul than does a spirit of gratitude and praise. It is a positive duty to resist melancholy, discontented thoughts and feelings—as much a duty as it is to pray. If we are heaven-bound, how can we go as a band of mourners, groaning and complaining all along the way to our Father's house?"

"Those professed Christians who are constantly complaining, and who seem to think cheerfulness and happiness a sin, have not genuine religion. Those who take a mournful pleasure in all that is melancholy in the natural world, who choose to look upon dead leaves rather than to gather the beautiful living flowers, who see no beauty in grand mountain heights and in valleys clothed with living green, who close their senses to the joyful voice which speaks to them in nature, and which is sweet and musical to the listening ear—these are not in Christ. They are gathering to themselves gloom and darkness, when they might have brightness, even the Sun of Righteousness arising in their hearts with healing in His beams."

"It is a law of nature that our thoughts and feelings are encouraged and strengthened as we give them utterance. While words express thoughts, it is also true that thoughts follow words. If we would give more expression to our faith, rejoice more in the blessings that we know we have,—the great mercy and love of God,—we should have more faith and greater joy. No tongue can express, no finite mind can conceive, the blessing that results from appreciating the goodness and love of God."

"Let the fresh blessings of each new day awaken praise in our hearts for these tokens of His loving care. When you open your eyes in the morning, thank God that He has kept you through the night. Thank Him for His peace in your heart. Morning, noon, and night, let gratitude as a sweet perfume ascend to heaven."

"One of the surest hindrances to the recovery of the sick is the centering of attention upon themselves. Many invalids feel that everyone should give them sympathy and help, when what they need is to have their attention turned away from themselves, to think of and care for others."

"Good deeds are twice a blessing, benefiting both the giver and the receiver of the kindness. The consciousness of right-doing is one of the best medicines for diseased bodies and minds. When the mind is free and happy from a sense of duty well done and the satisfaction of giving happiness to others, the cheering, uplifting influence brings new life to the whole being."

@TWEETS_OF_HEALING

The relation between the #mind & the #body is very intimate. When 1 is affected, the other sympathizes.

The condition of the #mind affects the #health 2 a far gr8er degree than many realize.

Many of the #diseases frm which #men suffer r the result of mental #depression.

Grief, anxiety, discontent, remorse, guilt, distrust, all tend 2 break down the #life forces & 2 invite decay & #death.

The 1 who made our #minds knows what they need.

Thr r many who make #life's burdens doubly heavy by continually anticipating trouble.

When care, perplexity & #darkness seem 2 surround ur #soul, look 2 the place where u last saw the #light.

Nothng tends 2 promote #health of #body & of #soul than does a #spirit of #gratitude & #praise.

Those professed @Christians, who seem 2 think that #cheerfulness & #happiness is a #sin, do not hve genuine #religion.

Those who take mournful #pleasure in all that is #melancholy in the #natural world, these r not in @Christ.

Our #thoughts & #feelings r encouraged & strengthened as we give them utterance.

Whl #words express #thoughts, it's also true that thoughts follow #words.

We cn educate our #hearts & lips 2 speak the #praise of @God for #His matchless #love.

We r not 2 dwell on the gr8 #power of @Satan. Let us talk abt the gr8 power of @God instead.

When tempted, instead of giving utterance 2 our #feelings, let us by #faith lift up a #songofthanksgiving 2 @God.

#Song is a weapon that we cn always use against discouragement.

One of the surest hindrances 2 the #recovery of the #sick is the centering of attention upon themselves.

@God answers #prayer for those who place themselves in the channel of #His #blessings.

#Good deeds r twice a #blessing, benefitting both the giver & the receiver of the #kindness.

DISCUSSION QUESTION

The concept of **human wholeness implies that there is an intimate relationship between the mind and the body.** The condition of the mind has a powerful effect on the health of the body. Psychology today speaks of "positive thinking."

1. What is "positive thinking" for a Christian? What does it include (according to this chapter)? Does Ellen White go "beyond" positive thinking only?

IN CONTACT WITH NATURE

CH. 19, PP. 261-268

SUMMARY

The Garden of Eden provides the model for the healthiest kind of environment. Nature and experiences with nature have great healing power for the sick.

THOUGHTS

In this period of Ellen White's life, her writings articulate a pair of initiatives that need to be read in balance with each other. On the one hand, there is the emphasis of this chapter on staying in close touch with nature as a fundamental principle of healing. On the other hand, there is a strong emphasis in many places on engagement with the large cities and the great needs there that would draw believers out of country settings. The danger of cities and the need of cities are both emphasized and the choice is left with readers as to how best to balance the two imperatives (whole chapter).

In today's world, this counsel needs to be read in the context of "all other things being equal." All other things being equal, the counsel of this chapter offers helpful guidelines to healing. But major changes in the world, such as massive urbanization, require one to balance this counsel with the requirements of a very different world than the one Ellen White originally wrote to.

All other things being equal, the sick need to be brought into close contact with nature. The great cities concentrate pollution, the spread of disease, confinement in surroundings that are often unlovely, and exposure to temptation. More natural settings provide fresher air, more access to sunshine, more availability of exercise, and uplifting landscapes. All other things being equal, the latter is more conducive to healing than the former. Natural settings are often more conducive to encounters with God as well.

NATURAL SETTINGS ARE OFTEN MORE CONDUCIVE TO ENCOUNTERS WITH GOD.

Counsel like this needs to be balanced with an awareness of God's love for the cities. While the Garden is the ideal at the beginning of the Bible, when Eden is restored it ends up as the holy city. In nineteenth-century America, people generally thought of the country as the ideal. There was a romantic notion of nature. But many people are inspired by the city. In the broadest sense, nature includes humans. Human beings are the apex of creation, and at their best cities reflect the creativity and organization that God has placed in humans. Not only that, in today's world it is "greener" to live in cities; you use more resources being spread out in the country.

If you are going to work in the city, you need to love the city or you won't be effective. God's people can do little things that improve the urban environment around them, like putting flowers in pots on the front stairs or in window boxes outside the apartment. While Ellen White loved nature, she didn't make a god out of nature. She also counseled that cities needed to be worked because that is where most of the people are.

QUOTABLE QUOTES

"The Creator chose for our first parents the surroundings best adapted for their health and happiness. He did not place them in a palace or surround them with the artificial adornments and luxuries that so many today are struggling to obtain. He placed them in close touch with nature and in close communion with the holy ones of heaven."

"Institutions for the care of the sick would be far more successful if they could be established away from the cities. And so far as possible, all who are seeking to recover health should place themselves amid country surroundings where they can have the benefit of outdoor life. . . . The pure air, the glad sunshine, the flowers and trees, the orchards and vineyards, and outdoor exercise amid these surroundings, are health-giving, life-giving."

"To the chronic invalid, nothing so tends to restore health and happiness as living amid attractive country surroundings. Here the most helpless ones can sit or lie in the sunshine or in the shade of the trees. They have only to lift their eyes to see above them the beautiful foliage. A sweet sense of restfulness and refreshing comes over them as they listen to the murmuring of the breezes. The drooping spirits revive. The waning strength is recruited. Unconsciously the mind becomes peaceful, the fevered pulse more calm and regular. As the sick grow stronger, they will venture to take a few steps to gather some of the lovely flowers, precious messengers of God's love to His afflicted family here below."

@TWEETS_OF_HEALING

The plan of #life which @God appointed for our first #parents has lessons for us.

The #sick need 2 b brought into close touch wt #nature.

When #patients r kept out of doors, they require less #care.

DISCUSSION QUESTION

Nature can be a great healing power for the sick. However, the reality is that today the **majority of people live in urban centers** (big cities).

1. How can we follow the principles given in this chapter today?

GENERAL HYGIENE

CH. 20, PP. 271-276

SUMMARY

Human beings are a temple for God, a dwelling where God's glory is to be revealed. This should provide the highest incentive to care for and develop our physical powers.

THOUGHTS

Since the body is a temple for God, this chapter encourages us to make it our study, to understand its needs, and to do all we can to preserve it from harm and defilement.

The temple was a symbol of purity in the ancient world. Ellen White translated this for today in very practical ways, such as cleanliness. Temples also involve the presence of God. Adventist self-supporting institutions consciously or unconsciously build on the purity idea, living far out in the country keeps you from being polluted by the city and the culture. Kellogg sought to apply the temple concept to the body in creative ways, thinking he was honoring a long-standing Adventist way of thinking, but pantheistic tendencies got him in trouble with Ellen White instead. Mormons also have a strong interest in temple purity issues, so this may be responding to a strong tendency in American culture at the time.

The basic thesis of the chapter is that in order to have good health we need to have "good blood." Good blood is defined as what you have when the blood is supplied with the proper food elements and when it is cleansed and vitalized by contact with pure air. The better the circulation, the better the blood can bring life and vigor to every part of the body. The concept of "bad blood" was used at the time for a wide range of maladies, so Ellen White's language here made sense at the time. Today we will want to focus on the larger principles and test the utility of the detailed particulars in an evidence-based way.

Circulation is hindered by tight clothing or insufficient clothing of the extremities of the body. The blood is cleansed and vitalized by deep breathing. Good breathing is hindered by stooping and tight lacing, among other things.

In the construction of buildings, care should be taken to provide for good ventilation and plenty of sunlight. As far as possible, buildings should be placed on high, well-drained ground. Sleeping rooms especially need to have free circulation of air day and night, while access to sunshine removes unhealthy dampness and mold.

Scrupulous cleanliness is essential to both physical and mental health. Both the body and the clothing needs to be kept clean so that the pores can do their job of throwing off waste matter.

Much of this chapter operates in the realm of what we call public health today.

QUOTABLE QUOTES

"The knowledge that man is to be a temple for God, a habitation for the revealing of His glory, should be the highest incentive to the care and development of our physical powers. Fearfully and wonderfully has the Creator wrought in the human frame, and He bids us make it our study, understand its needs, and act our part in preserving it from harm and defilement."

"In order to have good health, we must have good blood; for the blood is the current of life. It repairs waste and nourishes the body. When supplied with the proper food elements and when cleansed and vitalized by contact with pure air, it carries life and vigor to every part of the system."

"In the construction of buildings, whether for public purposes or as dwellings, care should be taken to provide for good ventilation and plenty of sunlight. Churches and schoolrooms are often faulty in this respect. Neglect of proper ventilation is responsible for much of the drowsiness and dullness that destroy the effect of many a sermon and make the teacher's work toilsome and ineffective."

"Perfect cleanliness, plenty of sunlight, careful attention to sanitation in every detail of the home life, are essential to freedom from disease and to the cheerfulness and vigor of the inmates of the home."

@TWEETS_OF_HEALING

In order 2 hve good #health, we must hve good #blood.

In order 2 hve good #blood, we must breathe well.

So far as possible, all #buildings intended for #human habitation should b placed on high, well-drained ground.

No #room is fit 2 b occupied as a #sleeping room unless it cn b thrown open daily 2 the air & #sunshine.

Scrupulous #cleanliness is essential 2 both physical & mental #health.

Lack of #cleanliness leads 2 #disease. #Germs abound in dark corners, decaying refuse, dampness, mold & must.

DISCUSSION QUESTIONS

Discuss: **How to Read Ellen White responsibly.**

- Context (historical vs. immediate)
- Principle vs. Application
- Real vs. Ideal

1. Can you give examples from the reading (for this week) where paying attention to the above applications may be helpful in order to understand Ellen White better?

   - p. 235—Vital force / life force
   - p. 291–293 (Dress)
   - p. 299 (Canning)

2. Why do you think this is important?

HYGIENE AMONG THE ISRAELITES

CH. 21, PP. 277-286

SUMMARY

The teaching God gave to Israel was designed to train them in habits that would help preserve their health. The clean and unclean distinctions played a major role in that. These teachings are also helpful to us.

THOUGHTS

In this chapter, the focus is on teaching the Israelites how to maintain the health of a large society that had recently been in slavery and ignorance. There are a lot of similarities between the laws of Moses and the concerns of public health today.

According to the chapter, the laws of clean and unclean had more than a religious purpose, they were intended also to assist in preserving health. Through the laws of clean and unclean, contagious and contaminating illnesses could be isolated from the Israelite encampment. Unsafe dwellings were to be destroyed. Personal cleanliness was to be practiced. Unwholesome foods were to be avoided.

This chapter also reminds us that a cheerful spirit, outdoor recreation, and a strong social life are essential to both physical and moral health.

It is probably helpful to note that most Jews and scholars of the Pentateuch (five books of Moses) do not see these laws as health laws, but rather points of ritual distinction between the Israelites and other people. So in sharing things from this chapter, don't expect Jews to be grateful. Rituals of various kinds are important to the unity and cohesion of a family or community. For example, the Adventist stand on alcoholic beverages (total abstinence) cannot be conclusively demonstrated from either the Bible or science, yet has great value on social grounds. While it can be argued that small amounts of alcohol in some contexts may have health benefits, the overall picture of alcohol in society is as destructive as any other negative social element.

THE LAWS OF CLEAN AND UNCLEAN HAD MORE THAN A RELIGIOUS PURPOSE, THEY WERE INTENDED ALSO TO ASSIST IN PRESERVING HEALTH.

QUOTABLE QUOTES

"In the teaching that God gave to Israel, the preservation of health received careful attention. The people who had come from slavery with the uncleanly and unhealthful habits which it engenders, were subjected to the strictest training in the wilderness before entering Canaan."

"Had the Israelites obeyed the instruction they received, and profited by their advantages, they would have been the world's object lesson of health and prosperity. If as a people they had lived according to God's plan, they would have been preserved from the diseases that afflicted other nations. Above any other people they would have possessed physical strength and vigor of intellect. They would have been the mightiest nation on the earth.

"The Israelites failed of fulfilling God's purpose, and thus failed of receiving the blessings that might have been theirs. But in Joseph and Daniel, in Moses and Elisha, and many others, we have noble examples of the results of the true plan of living. Like faithfulness today will produce like results."

@TWEETS_OF_HEALING

@Christ has warned us against the #pride of #life, bt not against its #grace & natural #beauty.

Gratitude, rejoicing, benevolence, #trust in @God's #love & #care—these r health's gr8est safeguard.

If as a ppl they had lived according 2 @God's plan, Israel would hve been preserved frm the #diseases that afflicted other #nations.

The #Israelites failed of fulfilling @God's #purpose & thus #failed of receiving the blessings that might hve been theirs.

DISCUSSION QUESTIONS

The laws of clean and unclean foods that God gave to the Israelites *had more than religious purposes only.* Their prime purpose was "health."

We, as the Adventist church of today have rules that we observe that are *not* "strictly" biblical but have health motivations.

Example: Not drinking wine and not smoking

1. How should we explain our motivations for doing certain things to the outside world? Why do we do them?

2. What is the main principle behind such "rules"?

3. The Israelites were to be an example for the other nations. How can we be a "living testament" of healthy living today? What do we need to do as individuals and as a church? Are we doing it? Where have we failed?

DRESS

CH. 22, PP. 287-294

SUMMARY

Ellen White's multitude of counsels on dress are here beautifully summarized in terms of large principles of action. In our choice of clothing, we will be greatly benefited by following principles of modesty, economy, simplicity, and healthfulness.

THOUGHTS

Immodesty is here defined as "any device designed to attract attention to the wearer or to excite admiration." This would no doubt include drawing attention with the absence of normal clothing!

Regarding economy, Ellen White notes that money is a trust from God. It should not be expended for the gratification of pride or ambition. Means that could bring happiness to others should not be expended for needless display.

The principle of simplicity is grounded in Jesus' statement regarding the "lilies of the field." Dress should be as simple and natural as possible in order to emphasize the "beautiful dress" we can wear upon the soul. This principle emphasizes the character of the wearer.

The rest of the chapter focuses on the principle of healthfulness, with further comments on the issue of how money is used. In following the latest fashions, our dress puts unnecessary pressure on the poorer classes who feel driven to keep up at the expense of health. Chasing after fashion also takes time that could be better spent preserving health, promoting character development, and fostering family relationships. Many fashions are themselves unhealthy, when they expose the body, burden it, or constrain it in ways that undermine health. Clearly, in Ellen White's day dress and health were conjoined issues. "Health Reform" was of a piece with "diet reform" as a means establishing and preserving health.

Such a principled approach is much more relevant to us today than the multitude of details that were aimed at specific situations more than a hundred years ago. Ellen White's detailed dress counsels need to be read in light of the principles in this chapter. When it comes to dress, principle is key, after all, Ellen White was encouraging shorter skirts, which today would not be either healthy or modest. So the principled approach of this chapter has enduring value.

A fun story. One faculty member of the School of Religion grew up in a state that was becoming concerned about the general deterioration in dress standards, not just in terms of modesty, but also in terms of appropriateness. They held a contest in the schools, encouraging the students to address how to raise the standards in that state by writing essays on the topic. As a school child, the young man researched what Ellen White wrote on the subject and shared it as an essay of his own, without indicating the source. He won the first prize, a brand-new suit of clothes! So these principles can be attractive even in mainstream society.

QUOTABLE QUOTES

"Money is a trust from God. It is not ours to expend for the gratification of pride or ambition. In the hands of God's children it is food for the hungry, and clothing for the naked. It is a defense to the oppressed, a means of health to the sick, a means of preaching the gospel to the poor. You could bring happiness to many hearts by using wisely the means that is now spent for show. Consider the life of Christ. Study His character, and be partakers with Him in His self-denial."

"But our clothing, while modest and simple, should be of good quality, of becoming colors, and suited for service. It should be chosen for durability rather than display. It should provide warmth and proper protection."

"(Dress) should have the grace, the beauty, the appropriateness of natural simplicity. Christ has warned us against the pride of life, but not against its grace and natural beauty. He pointed to the flowers of the field, to the lily unfolding in its purity, and said, 'Even Solomon in all his glory was not arrayed like one of these.' Matthew 6:29. Thus by the things of nature Christ illustrates the beauty that heaven values, the modest grace, the simplicity, the purity, the appropriateness, that would make our attire pleasing to Him."

"The most beautiful dress He bids us wear upon the soul. No outward adorning can compare in value or loveliness with that 'meek and quiet spirit' which in His sight is 'of great price.' 1 Peter 3:4."

@TWEETS_OF_HEALING

In the #hands of @God's #children #money is food for the #hungry & clothing for the #naked.

You cld bring happiness 2 many #hearts by using wisely the means that is now spent for show.

@Christ has warned us against the #pride of #life, bt not against its #grace & natural #beauty.

The most beautiful #clothing is that which @God bids us wear upon the #soul.

DISCUSSION QUESTIONS

Ellen White talks about modesty, fashion, display, and ornaments.

1. What is she really concerned with? Is she against "good-looking" young people? What does this mean for today?

2. Can modesty have extremes too (example: the Amish)?

DIET AND HEALTH

CH. 23, PP. 295–310

SUMMARY

The theme of this chapter could be "You are what you eat." Our bodies are built up from the food we eat, so careful selection and timing of the diet is a critical factor in overall health.

THOUGHTS

The foods chosen should be those that best supply the elements needed for building up the body. Appetite is not a safe guide in this process, but God's original plan for the human diet (in Genesis) is. This consisted of grains, fruits, nuts, and vegetables.

Not all wholesome foods, however, are suited to our needs in all circumstances. Diet should be suited to the season, the climate, and the occupation we follow. What is appropriate for one is not necessarily appropriate for another.

In the pages that follow, Ellen White gives a number of specific recommendations regarding nuts, fruits, grains (bread), dairy products, and sugar. There should not be a great variety at any one meal and meals should be taken at regular times (five or six hours between meals), nothing in between and nothing just before bedtime.

The science on many of these is mixed; for example, in some cases five or six small meals a day seems healthier than two or three with nothing in between. But the principle of individuality that is clearly articulated in this chapter is an appropriate caution to taking most or all of this counsel as hard and fast rules. Two meals a day does seem a bit challenging in today's world.

The chapter closes with a number of detailed suggestions regarding liquids, quantity, speed, attitude while eating, food preparation, and the Sabbath. On the last page is an important admonition that one cannot be a rule for another. Everyone needs to exercise reason and control and should act from principle.

Taken as a whole, Ellen White's counsels regarding diet are far more balanced than is the use of her counsels. *The Ministry of Healing* provides a counterweight to the focus on detailed rules of eating that arise from an unbalanced use of indexes and search engines to mine her writings. We need to keep in mind that she spoke to the times in which she lived. She does not address many issues that we face today (such as abortion and genetically modified foods). If a gene were drawn from a pig and increased grain yields, is the grain somehow defiled? Science is needed in the application of her principles today.

In raising the issue of modern scientific verification of her health principles, we should be careful not to put her prophetic mantle to the test in terms of every detail, some of which we may not fully understand. Her prophetic worth is demonstrable in the big things, things such as the founding of health-care work and Loma Linda, the decentralization of church structure, the worldwide focus on Adventist education. Her big idea in *The Ministry of Healing* is healthful living. Science can and should help us with the how. It has become generally recognized that vegetarianism has powerful positive implications both for world hunger (increases protein yield per acre) and for the environment (large-scale animal production increases carbon in the atmosphere). So her big ideas have huge implications for today's world.

A challenge with regard to Adventist health science is the tendency to manage the evidence so research will end up supporting her specifics. This not only includes highlighting evidence that seems to support but sometimes hiding evidence that seems to contradict. She herself would want us to follow the evidence honestly and openly.

QUOTABLE QUOTES

"Those foods should be chosen that best supply the elements needed for building up the body. In this choice, appetite is not a safe guide."

"Grains, fruits, nuts, and vegetables constitute the diet chosen for us

DIET SHOULD BE SUITED TO THE SEASON, THE CLIMATE, AND THE OCCUPATION WE FOLLOW.

by our Creator. These foods, prepared in as simple and natural a manner as possible, are the most healthful and nourishing."

"Often food that can be used with benefit by those engaged in hard physical labor is unsuitable for persons of sedentary pursuits or intense mental application. God has given us an ample variety of healthful foods, and each person should choose from it the things that experience and sound judgment prove to be best suited to his own necessities."

"Persons who have accustomed themselves to a rich, highly stimulating diet have an unnatural taste, and they cannot at once relish food that is plain and simple. . . . But those who persevere in the use of wholesome food will, after a time, find it palatable. Its delicate and delicious flavors will be appreciated, and it will be eaten with greater enjoyment than can be derived from unwholesome dainties."

"If the food eaten is not relished, the body will not be so well nourished. The food should be carefully chosen and prepared with intelligence and skill."

"To make food appetizing and at the same time simple and nourishing, requires skill; but it can be done. Cooks should know how to prepare simple food in a simple and healthful manner, and so that it will be found more palatable, as well as more wholesome, because of its simplicity."

"Regularity in eating is of vital importance. There should be a specified time for each meal. At this time let everyone eat what the system requires and then take nothing more until the next meal."

"When we lie down to rest, the stomach should have its work all done, that it, as well as the other organs of the body, may enjoy rest."

"By overeating on the Sabbath, many do more than they think to unfit themselves for receiving the benefit of its sacred opportunities."

"There are men and women of excellent natural ability who do not accomplish half what they might if they would exercise self-control in the denial of appetite.

"Many writers and speakers fail here. After eating heartily, they give themselves to sedentary occupations, reading, study, or writing, allowing no time for physical exercise. As a consequence the free flow of thought and words is checked. They cannot write or speak with the force and intensity necessary in order to reach the heart; their efforts are tame and fruitless."

"A disordered stomach produces a disordered, uncertain state of mind. Often it causes irritability, harshness, or injustice. Many a plan that would have been a blessing to the world has been set aside, many unjust, oppressive, even cruel measures have been carried, as the result of diseased conditions due to wrong habits of eating."

"Some wish that an exact rule could be prescribed for their diet. They overeat, and then regret it, and so they keep thinking about what they eat and drink. This is not as it should be. One person cannot lay down an exact rule for another. Everyone should exercise reason and self-control, and should act from principle."

@TWEETS_OF_HEALING

You r what u #eat.

Grains, fruits, nuts & vegetables constitute the #diet chosen for us by our #Creator.

Not all #wholesome #foods r equally suited 2 our needs under all circumstances.

Those who persevere in the use of #wholesome #foods will in #time find them palatable.

Thr is more #religion in a good loaf of #bread than many ppl think.

Regularity in #eating is of vital importance.

#Eatslowly & wt #cheerfulness.

A disordered #stomach produces a disordered #mind.

When it comes 2 #diet, 1 person cn not lay down an exact #rule for another.

DISCUSSION QUESTIONS

Read: *"Our diet should be suited to the season, to the climate in which we live, and to the occupation we follow."*

1. Why is this advice particularly important for medical professionals?

2. How can you explain to people that there is not "one right diet"?

3. What are some of the things (in relation to diet) that students struggle the most today? What do you struggle with the most? What can you do to change?

FLESH AS FOOD

CH. 24, PP. 311-317

SUMMARY

In choosing the food for Adam and Eve in the Garden, God made clear that the best human diet did not include animal food. By sending manna, He taught Israel the same thing.

THOUGHTS

Ellen White frequently used the Garden of Eden as the model for health practices in her time. The question is, To what extent is the Genesis ideal a permanent foundation for everything we do? Most men aren't in a position to work the soil today, for example. What parts of the Genesis story are models for us and what parts aren't?

In the wilderness, Israel demanded flesh food. In granting their request, God placed the allowance under careful restrictions (clean meats only and avoiding fat and blood) to limit the negative consequences. Nevertheless, the use of meat resulted in disease and death for thousands. It is surprising in this chapter how many different reasons Ellen White gives for avoiding meat in the diet.

Flesh food is best left alone because disease in animals is rapidly increasing. Swine are scavengers and full of parasites. Surprising, perhaps, is Ellen White's strong emphasis on the suffering of animals and the ethics of eating their flesh.

Ellen White also argues against the idea that meat is necessary for building muscular strength. She argues that grains, fruits, nuts, and vegetables contain all the properties necessary to maintain health and strength.

Having said all this, note her strong statements that we need to show compassion for those who struggle with this issue. She herself seems to have struggled with it. Circumstances alter cases.

Many of her arguments for vegetarianism are widely confirmed today, plus a couple of important new ones have arisen. Today it is widely understood that meat production is inefficient. Much plant food goes into animals to produce a relatively small amount of meat. This is not an efficient use of acreage. In addition, meat production is one of the biggest causes of atmospheric carbon and greenhouse gasses. So two major world problems could be largely resolved if most human beings ate a plant-based diet.

QUOTABLE QUOTES

"The diet appointed man in the beginning did not include animal food. Not till after the Flood, when every green thing on the earth had been destroyed, did man receive permission to eat flesh. In choosing man's food in Eden, the Lord showed what was the best diet; in the choice made for Israel He taught the same lesson."

"Those who eat flesh are but eating grains and vegetables at second hand; for the animal receives from these things the nutrition that produces growth. The life that was in the grains and vegetables passes into the eater. We receive it by eating the flesh of the animal. How much better to get it direct, by eating the food that God provided for our use!"

"The moral evils of a flesh diet are not less marked than are the physical ills. Flesh food is injurious to health, and whatever affects the body has a corresponding effect on the mind and the soul. Think of the cruelty to animals that meat-eating involves, and its effect on those who inflict and those who behold it. How it destroys the tenderness with which we should regard these creatures of God!"

"The intelligence displayed by many dumb animals approaches so closely to human intelligence that it is a mystery. The animals see and hear and love and fear and suffer. . . . They manifest sympathy and tenderness toward their companions in suffering. Many animals show an affection for those who have charge of them, far superior to the affection shown by some of the human race. They form attachments for man which are not broken without great suffering to them."

"We should, however, consider the situation of the people, and the power of lifelong habit, and be careful not to urge even right ideas unduly. None should be urged to make the change abruptly."

"In all cases educate the conscience, enlist the will, supply good, wholesome food, and the change will be readily made, and the demand for flesh will soon cease."

"Is it not time that all should aim to dispense with flesh foods? How can those who are seeking to become pure, refined, and holy, that they may have the companionship of heavenly angels, continue to use as food anything that has so harmful an effect on soul and body? How can they take the life of God's creatures that they may consume the flesh as a luxury? Let them, rather, return to the wholesome and delicious food given to man in the beginning, and themselves practice, and teach their children to practice, mercy toward the dumb creatures that God has made and has placed under our dominion."

@TWEETS_OF_HEALING

The #diet appointed #man in the beginning did not include #animal #food.

Those who #eat #flesh r bt eating grains & vegetables at second hand.

When it comes 2 #dietary chng, we should consider the situation of the ppl & not urge even right ideas unduly.

None should b urged 2 make #dietary chngs abruptly.

DISCUSSION QUESTIONS

Read: *"The Diet appointed man in the beginning did not include animal food. . . . In choosing man's food in Eden, the Lord showed what was the best diet"* (p. 311).

1. To what extend can the Genesis "ideal diet" be used as a model today? Why?
2. How does Ellen White apply the principle of a "vegetarian diet" to healthful living (see pp. 315, 316)?

EXTREMES IN DIET

CH. 25, PP. 318-324

SUMMARY

This chapter outlines some of the pitfalls on the way to dietary reform.

THOUGHTS

The chapter opens with a quick outline of three extremes in dietary reform. (1) Some discard selected unhealthy foods, but the rest of the diet remains the same. They don't understand the larger principles. (2) Others go to the opposite extreme and ban nearly everything, even if the resulting diet is unhealthy. (3) A third group opts for a simple diet but does not include the variety needed to supply the needs of the system. The bottom line is that a partial understanding of the principles of dietary reform can do more harm than good.

A major theme of the chapter is that dietary reform must be grounded in principles rather than specifics. Those operating by principle will avoid the extremes of indulgence and restriction. There needs to be a lot of common sense involved. Not all can eat the same things. What is palatable and wholesome to one can be harmful to another. Diet reform needs to be thought through and progressive.

Specific suggestions include two meals a day and where that makes sense, make your best choices and then be at peace. Don't scrimp on daily fare in order to have extra for entertaining. Food needs to be tasty as well as healthy, and everyone should have at least some knowledge of cooking.

Instead of being as different from others as possible, it is wiser to be as near as possible without the sacrifice of principle.

An important excursus on Ellen White's view of sexuality: On page 320, Ellen White uses the language of "animal passions" and "sensual habits." She does not seem to address the issue of sexuality anywhere else in *The Ministry of Healing,* so it may be wise to say something about it here. The language of "animal passions" is awkward today, as a Google search will confirm. In her mind, it probably meant a man allowing sexual urges to overpower the needs and feelings of his wife. Ellen White was not against sexual pleasure—there are no statements forbidding it directly. But she was certainly against a man using his wife for his own pleasure as if she were a prostitute. The following statement seems apropos to the meaning of her language: "No man can truly love his wife when she will patiently submit to become his slave and minister to his depraved passions. In her passive submission she loses the value she once possessed in his eyes. He sees her dragged down from everything elevating to a low level, and soon he suspects that she will as tamely submit to be degraded by another as by himself. . . . These men are worse than brutes; they are demons in human form" (*The Adventist Home,* 125). Her goal was not the stifling of marital pleasure but preservation of the value and dignity of the wife.

Some possible background information: In the Middle Ages, women were thought to be sexual creatures and men the controlled ones. If men were feeling or behaving in a lusty fashion, it was presumed that some woman cast a spell on them. In the Victorian period (when much of Ellen White's ministry occurred), the situation had reversed. Men were beasts and godly women needed to distract and attract them away from their brutish nature. This viewpoint helps explain some of the language Ellen White uses. Today the culture has shifted again. We encourage sexuality within the marriage bond, and some of her statements in another context can be perplexing.

According to a representative of the White Estate, much of Ellen White's still-unpublished writings (60–70 percent in his estimate) relate to the issue of sexual abuse. People didn't talk openly about such things in her day, but she addresses such issues frankly and personally in her correspondence. This helps explain her concern that certain food elements, like pepper, red meat, and coffee, might prove to be stimulants of the "animal passions." In today's world, aphrodisiacs, in food, herbs, and pharmaceuticals are sought after! As Ellen White herself often stated, circumstances alter cases. We read with open minds and hearts, but we also read with caution, lest we misunderstand or misinterpret and thereby cause needless pain and confusion.

QUOTABLE QUOTES

"Those who have but a partial understanding of the principles of reform are often the most rigid, not only in carrying out their views themselves, but in urging them on their families and their neighbors. The effect of their mistaken reforms, as seen in their own ill-health, and their efforts to force their views upon others, give many a false idea of dietetic reform, and lead them to reject it altogether."

"Those who understand the laws of health and who are governed by principle, will shun the extremes, both of indulgence and of restriction. Their diet is chosen, not for the mere gratification of appetite, but for the upbuilding of the body. They seek to preserve every power in the best condition for highest service to God and man. The appetite is under the control of reason and conscience, and they are rewarded with health of body and mind. While they do not urge their views offensively upon others, their example is a testimony in favor of right principles. These persons have a wide influence for good."

"There is real common sense in dietetic reform. The subject should be studied broadly and deeply, and no one should criticize others because their practice is not, in all things, in harmony with his own. It is impossible to make an unvarying rule to regulate everyone's habits, and no one should think himself a criterion for all. Not all can eat the same things. Foods that are palatable and wholesome to one person may be distasteful, and even harmful, to another."

"Some are continually anxious lest their food, however simple and healthful, may hurt them. To these let me say, Do not think that your food will injure you; do not think about it at all. Eat according to your best judgment; and when you have asked the Lord to bless the food for the strengthening of your body, believe that He hears your prayer, and be at rest."

"When those who advocate hygienic reform go to extremes, it is no wonder that many who regard these persons as representing health principles reject the reform altogether. These extremes frequently do more harm in a short time than could be undone by a lifetime of consistent living.

Hygienic reform is based upon principles that are broad and far-reaching, and we should not belittle it by narrow views and practices. . . . Those who are governed by principle will be firm and decided in standing for the right; yet in all their associations they will manifest a generous, Christlike spirit and true moderation."

@TWEETS_OF_HEALING

Not all who profess 2 #believe in dietetic reform r really #reformers.

Those who hve bt a partial understanding of the principles of #health #reform r often the most rigid.

Those who r governed by principle will shun the #extremes, both of #indulgence & of #restriction.

Not all cn #eat the same things.

#Diet #reform should b progressive.

An impoverished #diet produces poverty of the #blood.

All should learn what 2 #eat & how 2 cook it.

Keep #appetite under the control of #reason.

The narrow ideas of some would-be #health #reformers hve been a gr8 injury 2 the cause of #diet #reform.

DISCUSSION QUESTIONS

1. Ellen White's counsels regarding diet and health are far more balanced than some of the claims and the practices by some of her followers. What can be the reason for that? And why may this be the case? How can we help such followers of Ellen White?
2. How can you explain to people the difference between "principle" and "application" in the writings of Ellen White?

STIMULANTS AND NARCOTICS

CH. 26, PP. 325-335

SUMMARY

In this chapter, Ellen White expands the definition of stimulants and narcotics to include tea, coffee, mustard, pepper, spices, pickles, and anything that, in her terms, irritates the stomach.

THOUGHTS

In this chapter, Ellen White sees stimulants and narcotics at three different levels of harm. First and most harmful is alcohol and tobacco. Second is wine, beer, and fermented cider. Third are the condiments and stimulating drinks: tea, coffee, mustard, pepper, spices, and pickles. She felt that by indulging in these condiments and stimulating drinks the system develops a craving for things that are even more stimulating, like wine, liquor, and tobacco. She seems to see all of these acting on the system in a similar way, though to a different degree. She felt that all of these stimulants wear away the life forces and debilitate the system. And the condiments seem to function in her mind rather like "gateway drugs" to more serious stimulants.

Evidence-based science at the moment does not confirm the sentiments regarding tea, coffee, and condiments. In select cases, coffee is even prescribed for certain ailments. So the principle of "all things being equal" is certainly applicable to Ellen White's counsels on these matters and also the principle of individuality. What is harmful to one may be neutral or even helpful to another. Those who want to seriously follow Ellen White's counsel will study for themselves carefully and also be open to science. Where the use of some of these (coffee, tea, harsh spices) is indicated, moderation is nevertheless advisable. By the way, if there is medical reason to use coffee it might best be used black, as the addition of much cream and sugar would do more harm than good.

BY INDULGENCE OF PERVERTED APPETITE PEOPLE LOSE THEIR POWER TO RESIST TEMPTATION.

By way of perspective, spices in Ellen White's day were used in high quantities to preserve foods, especially meats. This may have played a role in the strength of her opinions on this. That would also underline the importance of moderation in their use, if used at all.

Certainly her comments on alcohol and tobacco are strongly supported by the evidence of both science and experience. She spends more time talking about cider than we would today. She denies that wine is ever sanctioned in the Bible or that Jesus produced alcoholic wine at the marriage feast in Cana.

Toward the end of the chapter, the focus turns to family dynamics. The key to the promotion of temperance is to reach the youth, and this is best handled at an early age and in the home. But temperance reform should not be limited to the home. Education is critical. The core principle is that the right balance of the mental and moral powers depends to a large extent on the right condition of the physical system. By indulgence of perverted appetite people lose their power to resist temptation.

The concluding paragraph has an interesting element. Ellen White includes tea, coffee, and all alcoholic drinks under the dictum of "touch not, taste not, handle not." But she does not mention the condiments here. Does this suggest that an absolute prohibition in the case of condiments is not realistic and that current practice of some use at most Adventist tables is not in violation of her strong statements in this chapter?

QUOTABLE QUOTES

"Men seek the excitement of stimulants, because, for the time, the results are agreeable. But there is always a reaction. The use of unnatural stimulants always tends to excess, and it is an active agent in promoting physical degeneration and decay."

"Nature needs time to recuperate her exhausted energies. When her forces are goaded on by the use of stimulants, more will be accomplished for a time; but, as the system becomes debilitated by their constant use, it gradually becomes more difficult to rouse the energies to the desired point. The demand for stimulants becomes more difficult to control, until the will is overborne and there seems to be no power to deny the unnatural craving. Stronger and still stronger stimulants are called for, until exhausted nature can no longer respond."

"To what extent can one indulge the liquor habit and be safely trusted with the lives of human beings? He can be trusted only as he totally abstains.

"Intoxication is just as really produced by wine, beer, and cider as by stronger drinks. The use of these drinks awakens the taste for those that are stronger, and thus the liquor habit is established. Moderate drinking is the school in which men are educated for the drunkard's career. Yet so insidious is the work of these milder stimulants that the highway to drunkenness is entered before the victim suspects his danger."

"Often intemperance begins in the home. By the use of rich, unhealthful food the digestive organs are weakened, and a desire is created for food that is still more stimulating. Thus the appetite is educated to crave continually something stronger."

"There would soon be little necessity for temperance crusades if in the youth who form and fashion society, right principles in regard to temperance could be implanted."

"It must be kept before the people that the right balance of the mental and moral powers depends in a great degree on the right condition of the physical system. All narcotics and unnatural stimulants that enfeeble and degrade the physical nature tend to lower the tone of the intellect and morals. Intemperance lies at the foundation of the moral depravity of the world. By the indulgence of perverted appetite, man loses his power to resist temptation."

"Those who attempt to leave off these stimulants will for a time feel a loss and will suffer without them. But by persistence they will overcome the craving and cease to feel the lack. Nature may require a little time to recover from the abuse she has suffered; but give her a chance, and she will again rally and perform her work nobly and well."

@TWEETS_OF_HEALING

The continued use of nerve irritants wears away the #life forces.

The use of #tobacco is inconvenient, expensive, uncleanly, defiling 2 the user & offensive 2 others.

The unhealthful practices of past #generations affect the #children & youth of 2day.

No #human being needs #tobacco, bt multitudes r perishing for lack of the means that by its use is worse than wasted.

To what extent cn 1 indulge the #liquor habit & b safely trusted wt the lives of other #human beings?

The #wine that @Christ made frm #water at the marriage feast of cn a was the #pure juice of the grape.

Often intemperance begins in the #home.

The right #balance of the mental & moral #powers depends in a gr8 degree on the right condition of the #physical system.

In relation 2 tea, coffee, tobacco & alcoholic drinks, the only safe course is 2 #touch not, #taste not, handle not.

DISCUSSION QUESTIONS

1. Science is clear that tobacco is dangerous to health. However, science is less clear about the harmful effects of tea and coffee (and even moderate wine drinking). If true, what do you do with such facts from a medical perspective? Do you see a bigger principle?
2. Should we as Christians (or as a church) be involved in the promotion and establishment of laws that "prohibit" smoking or drinking in public places? Why or why not?
   - Example: Dr. Geshanova—Sofia, Bulgaria.

LIQUOR TRAFFIC AND PROHIBITION

CH. 27, PP. 337-346

SUMMARY

Healing ministry does not end with individuals; a strong work of social justice is needed to deal with the entrenched powers of the liquor industry, which brings wealth to a few and great wretchedness to many.

THOUGHTS

This chapter is the strongest argument in favor of social justice in the book so far. Ellen White argues that the liquor business is sheer robbery. For the money received, no equivalent value is returned. Instead the dollars spent on liquor bring only a curse to the spender.

Behind the sale of liquor is the working of Satan. The consequences of the production and consumption of alcohol include prostitution, crime, child and spouse abuse, mental and physical illness, colonial control over non-Christian populations, and all sorts of addictions. The liquor industry not only supplies the product but uses all sorts of snares to market it to those not yet ensnared.

Ellen White argues that the church shares responsibility for the degradation caused by alcohol when it accepts members involved in the liquor trade and donations of money raised by the manufacture and sale of alcohol.

The church also bears responsibility when it does not protest government licensing and regulation of the alcohol industry. The social costs of alcohol production and consumption are so great that the church cannot afford to be silent in the face of social and governmental support for the industry.

ELLEN WHITE SEEMS TO BE PROMOTING PROHIBITION OF PRODUCTION AND CONSUMPTION.

Ellen White's passion for this topic is evidenced by her support for the Women's Christian Temperance Union, for which she would often speak. Ironically, and as evidence for Ellen White's flexibility, the WCTU at the same time was supporting Sunday laws in the United States. Ellen White did not fear guilt by association when the issue was important to her.

There is no nuance in this chapter. The great degradation that results from alcoholism generates some strong language. In utilizing these perspectives, we should remember that a significant number of people who use alcohol use it in moderation and don't display most of the destructive tendencies of the alcoholic.

In Ellen White's day, slavery and anti-tobacco and anti-alcohol crusades were natural allies in the battle for societal reform. A possible parallel today is the gun industry. Would she say that gun manufacturers are responsible for the deaths their products cause? Drinking and driving is another contemporary area where a consensus for social reform may be possible.

In this chapter, Ellen White seems to be promoting prohibition of production and consumption. Was Prohibition ultimately a plus or a minus for the nation as a whole? It would be interesting to study whether more people were killed annually by the mafia during Prohibition or annually by alcohol before and since. One also has to balance the good that would come from reducing alcohol production and consumption with the huge police resources that might be needed to enforce some sort of prohibition today. A more productive approach might be how government has effectively reduced tobacco consumption through restricting the locations where smoking can occur and social pressure (public service announcements). One cannot overstate the evil of mass media showing young, athletic types on the beach enjoying alcohol. This makes alcohol socially acceptable, and regulating the intentional and unintentional promotion of alcohol is a direction where constructive change can occur. In spite of its social acceptance, alcohol is the most abused narcotic today.

In Ellen White's day, temperance and abstinence were not as sharply distinguished as they are today. The two ideas often meant the same thing. When she uses the term "temperance" it often means abstinence. But moderation in good things is also important.

QUOTABLE QUOTES

"Houses of prostitution, dens of vice, criminal courts, prisons, almshouses, insane asylums, hospitals, all are, to a great degree, filled as a result of the liquor seller's work. Like the mystic Babylon of the Apocalypse, he is dealing in "slaves, and souls of men." Behind the liquor seller stands the mighty destroyer of souls, and every art which earth or hell can devise is employed to draw human beings under his power."

"The licensing of the liquor traffic is advocated by many as tending to restrict the drink evil. But the licensing of the traffic places it under the protection of law. The government sanctions its existence, and thus fosters the evil which it professes to restrict. Under the protection of license laws, breweries, distilleries, and wineries are planted all over the land, and the liquor seller plies his work beside our very doors."

"Less harmful would it be to grant liquor to the confirmed drunkard, whose ruin, in most cases, is already determined, than to permit the flower of our youth to be lured to destruction through this terrible habit."

"Considering only the financial aspect of the question, what folly it is to tolerate such a business! But what revenue can compensate for the loss of human reason, for the defacing and deforming of the image of God in man, for the ruin of children, reduced to pauperism and degradation, to perpetuate in their children the evil tendencies of their drunken fathers?"

"It is not the drunkard and his family alone who are imperiled by the work of the liquor seller, nor is the burden of taxation the chief evil which his traffic brings on the community. We are all woven together in the web of humanity. The evil that befalls any part of the great human brotherhood brings peril to all."

@TWEETS_OF_HEALING

Behind the #liquor seller stands the mighty destroyer of #souls.

Little #children r in daily peril thru the neglect, the abuse, the vileness of drunken #mothers.

Frm the so-called @Christian lands the curse of #alcohol is carried 2 the #world. The #West is hated because of this.

#Churches that accept members who wrk in the #liquor industry r virtually sustaining the #liquor traffic.

The #government sanctions the #liquor industry's existence & thus fosters the #evil which it professes 2 restrict.

The #government that licenses the #liquor seller should b held responsible for the results of his traffic.

The #evil that befalls any part of the gr8 #human brotherhood brings peril 2 all.

Thr is no #man whose interests the #liquor traffic does not imperil.

DISCUSSION QUESTIONS

1. Some stats show that drinking moderate amounts of alcohol may be healthy. Is that true? And how do we validate such stats with what Ellen White is saying?
2. Based on the principles developed in this chapter, what should be our stand on the question of "legalizing marijuana"?
   - Example: the Colorado law and its implications.

MINISTRY OF THE HOME

CH. 28, PP. 349-355

SUMMARY

The home is the greatest single influence for good in the world. The future of youth is largely decided there for good or evil. Besides the upbringing of children, the home is to be a blessing to outcasts, strangers, and youth who would otherwise go down to ruin.

THOUGHTS

The thesis of this chapter is that society is whatever the leaders of the home make it. Through the upbringing of children, parents have more to do with the outcomes of community, church, and nation than any other influence. The outcomes in Jesus' life are a good illustration of the importance of home training.

Great efforts are put forth to reform the victims of evil habits. But such reform is much more difficult to obtain in the settled lives of adults than it is with children and youth. Training of parents treats these problems more effectively, dealing with "the stream" at its source.

In addition to training the children, the mission of the home extends beyond the family to the poor, the stranger, church workers, and in particular troubled youth who don't have the kind of adult influences in their lives that they need. Parents can accomplish this work through a kindly, self-sacrificing spirit and a steadfast purpose.

This chapter and the following address the norm for the home in the late nineteenth century. The norm then was two-parent families raising children in proximity with aunts, uncles, and grandparents. One could call this the extended nuclear family. Today's extended families are split apart geographically and often even the nuclear family is divided by work or "unreconcilable differences." Implementing her counsel in detail in most cases would be radically more difficult than a hundred years ago. It is extremely difficult and stressful to raise children well in two-income families that are separated from their extended family.

Interestingly, Ellen White herself had what we might call a "stressful home." Personal letters indicate that there was considerable tension during many periods of their marriage between her and her husband. Her work often separated her from her children and at least two of her sons had serious "teenage" issues. What she writes about here is an ideal, one that she herself was struggling to reach. Knowing this can mitigate the tension for self-judgment and discouragement that afflicts many who read these lines.

Every generation has tended to decry the decline of the family in its time. Yet do we really want to go back to a time when there was no Internet, no automobile, no cell phones, no air travel, et cetera? Is that even possible? Perhaps we need to adapt the principles of this chapter and find new ways to accomplish them in the context of life today. The basic principle of the chapter seems to be something like, "spend time with children." Through Skype, Facetime, and Facebook, for example, extended families and even separated nuclear families can maintain much closer contact than was possible even ten years ago. Church communities can learn how to function as "aunties and uncles" and surrogate grandparents to new generations who desperately need them. Radical principles sometimes require radical solutions.

QUOTABLE QUOTES

"The restoration and uplifting of humanity begins in the home. The work of parents underlies every other. Society is composed of families, and is what the heads of families make it. Out of the heart are "the issues of life" (Proverbs 4:23); and the heart of the community, of the church, and of the nation is the household. The well-being of society, the success of the church, the prosperity of the nation, depend upon home influences."

"The Saviour's early years are more than an example to the youth. They are a lesson, and should be an encouragement, to every parent. . . . No

EVERY GENERATION HAS TENDED TO DECRY THE DECLINE OF THE FAMILY IN ITS TIME.

work entrusted to human beings involves greater or more far-reaching results than does the work of fathers and mothers."

"It is by the youth and children of today that the future of society is to be determined, and what these youth and children shall be depends upon the home. To the lack of right home training may be traced the larger share of the disease and misery and crime that curse humanity. If the home life were pure and true, if the children who went forth from its care were prepared to meet life's responsibilities and dangers, what a change would be seen in the world!"

"Parents may lay for their children the foundation for a healthy, happy life. They may send them forth from their homes with moral stamina to resist temptation, and courage and strength to wrestle successfully with life's problems. They may inspire in them the purpose and develop the power to make their lives an honor to God and a blessing to the world. They may make straight paths for their feet, through sunshine and shadow, to the glorious heights above."

"If we would show an interest in the youth, invite them to our homes, and surround them with cheering, helpful influences, there are many who would gladly turn their steps into the upward path."

"The work to which we are called does not require wealth or social position or great ability. It requires a kindly, self-sacrificing spirit and a steadfast purpose. . . . If we will open our hearts and homes to the divine principles of life we shall become channels for currents of life-giving power. From our homes will flow streams of healing, bringing life and beauty and fruitfulness where now are barrenness and dearth."

@TWEETS_OF_HEALING

The restoration & uplifting of #humanity begins in the #home.

The well-being of society, the success of the #church, the prosperity of the #nation, depend upon #home influences.

#Society is composed of #families & is what the heads of families make it.

No wrk entrusted 2 #human beings involves more far-reaching results than does the wrk of #fathers & #mothers.

The lack of right #home training causes the larger share of the #disease & misery & #crime that curse #humanity.

Far more powerful than any #sermon is the influence of a true #home upon #human hearts & #lives.

If we will open our #hearts & #homes 2 the #divine principles of #life, streams of healing will flow frm our #homes.

The #home is the gr8est single influence for #good in the #world.

DISCUSSION QUESTIONS

1. In chapters 28–34, Ellen White deals with a number of issues related to marriage, the home, and raising children. A contemporary issue upon which she is understandably silent is the issue of gay marriage. This raises the interesting question, If Ellen White were alive today, what counsel would she offer regarding the political and moral issues related to gay marriage? Why would she say what you think she would say?
2. How should health care workers address alternate types of families (same-sex parents, single moms and dads, transgender people, etc.)?

THE **BUILDERS** OF THE **HOME**

CH. 29, PP. 356-362

SUMMARY

The focus of this chapter is on marriage: how to choose a spouse, what to do when the romance wears off, and how to build a love that will last a lifetime.

THOUGHTS

Christ especially honored marriage in two ways: by performing His first miracle at a marriage festival and by making marriage a symbol of the union between Him and His redeemed ones (Eph. 5).

Marriage was designed to be a blessing to the whole human race, so it should be entered into with great care and thoughtful consideration. The first step in this consideration is to make the best possible choice, considering the potential partner's attitudes, character, physical and mental vigor, and relation to God. Where available, parents should be consulted.

While love is not a feeling but a principle, a marriage with no passion isn't much fun. So this statement needs to be combined with the thoughts on page 360, which indicate that feelings do matter. We need to study how to advance each other's happiness (a feeling) and continue "the early attentions."

Having made a choice and entered into marriage, the next key step is dealing with the disillusionment that inevitably comes when the romance wears off and the two parties are seen in their true character. At this point, it is critical that each party focuses on the excellencies discovered in each other rather than the defects and weaknesses. Love needs to be expressed over and over in kindness, sympathy, and the self-sacrificing forgiveness of Christ. The kind of focus on each other that lovers give naturally during the romance stage needs to be exercised in the long run by choice.

MARRIAGE WAS DESIGNED TO BE A BLESSING TO THE WHOLE HUMAN RACE.

But even the best of marriages can get stuck in a focus on each other. Ultimately, happiness is found when the couple reaches out to others in unselfish service. Service is an important component of a sound marriage.

An important part of the worldview that is implied in this chapter is that there is a lot of continuity between this world and the world to come. The present is not completely annihilated when Jesus comes. The bodily resurrection means that what we do with the body (and by extension our homes and relationships) matters for eternity. There is continuity. This worldview explains the Adventist ability to combine social action in this world with an apocalyptic pessimism about where the world is going. What we do now matters for eternity.

A brief comment on page 360, "Let neither husband nor wife harbor the thought that their union is a mistake or a disappointment." She does not say "never entertain the thought" or "never allow the thought to enter your mind," but do not "harbor the thought." In the real world, such thoughts may come to mind, but they are not to be "harbored" or dwelt on.

QUOTABLE QUOTES

"The family tie is the closest, the most tender and sacred, of any on earth. It was designed to be a blessing to mankind. And it is a blessing wherever the marriage covenant is entered into intelligently, in the fear of God, and with due consideration for its responsibilities."

"Those who are contemplating marriage should consider what will be the character and influence of the home they are founding. As they become parents, a sacred trust is committed to them. Upon them depends in a great measure the well-being of their children in this world, and their happiness in the world to come. To a great extent they determine both the physical and the moral stamp that the little ones receive. And upon the character of the home depends the condition of society; the weight of each family's influence will tell in the upward or the downward scale."

"The choice of a life companion should be such as best to secure physical, mental, and spiritual well-being for parents and for their children—such as will enable both parents and children to bless their fellow men and to honor their Creator."

"Love is a precious gift, which we receive from Jesus. Pure and holy affection is not a feeling, but a principle. Those who are actuated by true love are neither unreasonable nor blind."

"Let those who are contemplating marriage weigh every sentiment and watch every development of character in the one with whom they think to unite their life destiny. Let every step toward a marriage alliance be characterized by modesty, simplicity, sincerity, and an earnest purpose to please and honor God. Marriage affects the afterlife both in this world and in the world to come. A sincere Christian will make no plans that God cannot approve."

"Let a young woman accept as a life companion only one who possesses pure, manly traits of character, one who is diligent, aspiring, and honest, one who loves and fears God. Let a young man seek one to stand by his side who is fitted to bear her share of life's burdens, one whose influence will ennoble and refine him, and who will make him happy in her love."

"Love cannot long exist without expression. Let not the heart of one connected with you starve for the want of kindness and sympathy. Though difficulties, perplexities, and discouragements may arise, let neither husband nor wife harbor the thought that their union is a mistake or a disappointment. Determine to be all that it is possible to be to each other. Continue the early attentions."

"Make Christ first and last and best in everything. As your love for Him becomes deeper and stronger, your love for each other will be purified and strengthened. The spirit that Christ manifests toward us is the spirit that husband and wife are to manifest toward each other."

"Neither the husband nor the wife should attempt to exercise over the other an arbitrary control. Do not try to compel each other to yield to your wishes."

"But remember that happiness will not be found in shutting yourselves up to yourselves, satisfied to pour out all your affection upon each other. Seize upon every opportunity for contributing to the happiness of those around you. Remember that true joy can be found only in unselfish service."

@TWEETS_OF_HEALING

The #family tie is the closest, the most tender & sacred, of any on #earth.

Those considering #marriage should consider the character & influence of the #home they will b founding.

Upon the character of the #home depends the condition of #society.

It is only in @Christ that a #marriage alliance cn safely b formed.

#Love is a precious #gift that we receive frm @Jesus.

Pure & #holy affection is not a feeling, bt a #principle.

A sincere @Christian will make no plans that @God cn not approve.

Continue the early attentions after the #marriage as well as b4.

Let not the #heart of 1 connected wt u starve for the want of #kindness & sympathy.

Nvr harbor the thought that ur #marriage is a mistake.

When it comes 2 #marriage, let each give #love rther than exact it.

Make @Christ first & last & best in everything.

As ur #love for @Christ bcomes deeper & stronger, ur #love for each other will b purified & strengthened.

The #spirit that @Christ manifests toward us is the #spirit that #husband & #wife r 2 manifest toward each other.

True #joy cn b found only in unselfish #service.

DISCUSSION QUESTIONS

1. Do you agree with the idea that spouses should never harbor the thought that their marriage was a mistake? What about contexts in which there is abuse and violence? Is this an absolute rule or a general principle to be followed in most cases?
2. Summarize the various steps Ellen White encourages to ensure that marriage will be the blessing that it was designed by God to be (pages 356–362).

CHOICE AND PREPARATION OF THE HOME

CH. 30, PP. 363-370

SUMMARY

The ultimate purpose of our homes on earth is to be a symbol of and preparation for the heavenly home.

THOUGHTS

The location of the home should be decided on the basis of what will best aid preparation for the heavenly home. Life in the cities is complex, false, artificial, and full of temptations. These temptations have an almost irresistible power on youth. In addition to the distractions and temptations, cities are often a peril to health on account of crowding and pollution.

The life of Jesus and many Bible characters encourages us to choose simple houses, relatively free of display. The best home life is in a country setting characterized by simplicity, physical labor, service to others, and daily encounter with some hardship and difficulty. Youth should learn to work rather than spend their time amusing themselves. Better than any wealth you can pass on to your children is the gift of a healthy body, a sound mind, and a noble character.

Elaborate and expensive furnishings are not only costly, but they require extra effort to maintain. Through the exercise of good taste, simple and economical furnishing can make a home attractive and inviting.

A yard with lawn and flowers will do more to bring happiness to the household than expensive furnishings.

Ellen White exhibits a strong tendency in her day to prefer the country over the city for reasons well expressed in this chapter. But today country living is not as ready an option as it was one hundred years ago. Back then 80 percent of people lived in the country, soon 80 percent will live in urban areas. So some reflection on how to approach this counsel today should be of value.

Cities are concentrations of humanity in all its aspects. Cities concentrate the bad and the ugly, they also concentrate the good and the beautiful. Cities contain libraries, museums, great universities, beautiful architecture, and spectacular gardens. In these things one catches a glimpse of the human potential granted in the image of God. On the other hand, cities also concentrate the darkness of the human condition, vice, corruption, crime, squalor, and artificiality.

In a perfect world, perhaps, all could choose to live in country places. But if everyone tried to do so today, it would be an ecological disaster, eliminating forests and wilderness areas in favor of human residences. On the other hand, the mass farming methods that enable most people to live in cities concentrate food production in the hands of a powerful few and also challenge the environment. So there is often no perfect answer to the question of, Where shall I live? All other things being equal, follow the guidelines in this chapter. When things are not equal, follow to the best of your ability in that situation.

The above summary and this chapter are ideals. The Bible is full of godly characters who had dysfunctional families. Grace and patience are needed as we all seek to emulate the ideal.

QUOTABLE QUOTES

"The gospel is a wonderful simplifier of life's problems. Its instruction, heeded, would make plain many a perplexity and save us from many an error. It teaches us to estimate things at their true value and to give the most effort to the things of greatest worth—the things that will endure."

"Better than any other inheritance of wealth you can give to your children will be the gift of a healthy body, a sound mind, and a noble character."

"Instead of dwelling where only the works of men can be seen, where the sights and sounds frequently suggest thoughts of evil, where turmoil and confusion bring weariness and disquietude, go where you can look upon the works of God. . . . Go where, apart from the distractions and dissipations of city life, you can give your children your companionship, where you can teach them to learn of God through His works, and train them for lives of integrity and usefulness."

"Our artificial habits deprive us of many blessings and much enjoyment, and unfit us for living the most useful lives. Elaborate and expensive furnishings are a waste not only of money, but of that which is a thousandfold more precious. They bring into the home a heavy burden of care and labor and perplexity."

THE LOCATION OF THE HOME SHOULD BE DECIDED ON THE BASIS OF WHAT WILL BEST AID PREPARATION FOR THE HEAVENLY HOME.

"Furnish your home with things plain and simple, things that will bear handling, that can be easily kept clean, and that can be replaced without great expense. By exercising taste, you can make a very simple home attractive and inviting, if love and contentment are there."

@TWEETS_OF_HEALING

The #gospel is a wonderful simplifier of #life's problems.

The #home on #earth is 2 b a symbol of & a preparation for the #home in #heaven.

The #gospel teaches us 2 estimate things at their true #value & 2 give the most effort 2 the things of gr8est #worth.

An #expensive dwelling, elaborate furnishings, display, luxury & ease, do not furnish the conditions essential 2 a happy, useful #life.

Better than any other inheritance is the #gift of a healthy #body, a sound mind & a noble #character.

Our artificial #habits deprive us of many #blessings & much enjoyment & unfit us for #living the most useful #lives.

Elaborate & #expensive furnishings r not only costly, bt they require extra effort 2 maintain.

@God #loves the beautiful. He desires us 2 surround our #homes wt the beauty of #natural things.

A yard wt lawn & flowers will do more 2 bring #happiness 2 the household than expensive furnishings.

By exercising #taste, u cn make a very simple #home attractive & inviting.

DISCUSSION QUESTIONS

1. What impact should this chapter have on the choice of home locations in today's world? Is the counsel in this chapter also applicable to the choice of where to locate a health care practice? In what way?
2. Under what circumstances would "elaborate and expensive furnishings" or landscapes (pages 367–370) be more appropriate than others? Are there elements of Ellen White's counsel in this chapter that are no longer applicable? Why?

THE MOTHER

CH. 31, PP. 371-378

SUMMARY

The basic principle affirmed in this chapter is: "What the parents are, to a great extent, the children will be." While the primary focus of the chapter is on the mother, there are some comments also on the father's role, particularly during pregnancy.

THOUGHTS

The parents' physical conditions, their dispositions and appetites, and their mental and moral tendencies are, to a greater or lesser degree reproduced in their children. In cultivating the best in themselves, parents exert also a positive influence upon future generations. Parents need to do all they can to help children overcome temptation and make constructive choices as they grow up.

Ellen White places special responsibility upon the mother. The time of pregnancy is of particular concern as the child is not only nourished by the mother physically, but also mentally, emotionally, and spiritually. Mothers, therefore, need to guard their habits and include the well-being of the children, born and unborn, in their life choices. Particular care needs to be taken during pregnancy.

Along with avoiding dietary items that would diminish physical or mental strength, mothers should avoid overwork. Here is where fathers can help or hinder in particular. Fathers should do all they can to lessen the

PARENTS STAND IN THE PLACE OF GOD TO THEIR CHILDREN.

mother's burdens so she can concentrate on the health and character development of the children.

Both mothers and fathers need to maintain a cheerful and contented disposition. This will strengthen the vital force in the children as well as the parents.

Parenting may seem trivial and unrewarding, at times, but it is a great privilege and responsibility. No other work is of equal importance. Parents stand in the place of God to their children.

A helpful corollary to the emphases of this chapter could be "Parenting Isn't Easy!" It is good to be pointed in the right direction and motivated to comply, but it is also easy to become discouraged when we fail. To some degree all parents fail, so the gospel needs to be kept before us as we explore this topic.

It is interesting that Ellen White says relatively little about the role of fathers, and most of what she does say is more about husbands than fathers! This seems to reflect the era in which she writes, which was focused more on nurture than on genetics. Were she writing today, one wonders if she would also have more to say about the influence of culture and the how government regulations can help or hinder the health of the family.

The quote from page 378 listed below is one of the most lyrical in all of her writings. Enjoy!

QUOTABLE QUOTES

"What the parents are, that, to a great extent, the children will be. The physical conditions of the parents, their dispositions and appetites, their mental and moral tendencies, are, to a greater or less degree, reproduced in their children. The nobler the aims, the higher the mental and spiritual endowments, and the better developed the physical powers of the parents, the better will be the life equipment they give their children. In cultivating that which is best in themselves, parents are exerting an influence to mold society and to uplift future generations."

"The well-being of the child will be affected by the habits of the mother. Her appetites and passions are to be controlled by principle."

"If the mother unswervingly adheres to right principles, if she is temperate and self-denying, if she is kind, gentle, and unselfish, she may give her child these same precious traits of character."

"But at this time above all others she should avoid, in diet and in every other line, whatever would lessen physical or mental strength. By the command of God Himself she is placed under the most solemn obligation to exercise self-control."

"In life's toilsome way let the husband and father 'lead on softly,' as the companion of his journey is able to endure. Amidst the world's eager rush for wealth and power, let him learn to stay his steps, to comfort and support the one who is called to walk by his side."

"The mother should cultivate a cheerful, contented, happy disposition. Every effort in this direction will be abundantly repaid in both the physical well-being and the moral character of her children. A cheerful spirit will promote the happiness of her family and in a very great degree improve her own health."

"Great is the honor and the responsibility placed upon fathers and mothers, in that they are to stand in the place of God to their children. Their character, their daily life, their methods of training, will interpret His words to the little ones. Their influence will win or repel the child's confidence in the Lord's assurances."

"No other work can equal (the faithful mother's) in importance. She has not, like the artist, to paint a form of beauty upon canvas, nor, like the sculptor, to chisel it from marble. She has not, like the author, to embody a noble thought in words of power, nor, like the musician, to express a beautiful sentiment in melody. It is hers, with the help of God, to develop in a human soul the likeness of the divine."

@TWEETS_OF_HEALING

What the #parents are, that, 2 a gr8 extent, the #children will be.

In cultivating the best in themselves, #parents exert also a positive influence upon #future generations.

The well-being of the #child will b affected by the habits of the #mother.

If the #mother is temperate, self-denying, kind & unselfish, she may give her #child these same precious traits of #character.

During pregnancy, the #mother should avoid whatever would lessen physical or mental #strength.

The #mother should cultivate a cheerful, contented, happy disposition.

A cheerful #spirit will promote the happiness of the #mother's family & in a very gr8 degree improve her own #health.

#Fathers & #mothers stand in the place of @God 2 their #children.

No other wrk cn equal, in importance, the wrk of a faithful #mother.

DISCUSSION QUESTIONS

1. Some of the statements in this chapter are quite prescriptive and can be discouraging for a harried mother to read. How do you handle such statements? What balancing concepts do you find elsewhere in Ellen White's writings?
2. This chapter offers a strong defense of the concept of pre-natal influence in the relationship between the mother and the developing child. Based on your own reading and experience, to what degree is this counsel confirmed by both science and experience today?

THE CHILD

CH. 32, PP. 379-387

SUMMARY

This chapter covers much of the same ground as the previous chapter but focuses less on the parents and more on the child.

THOUGHTS

In chapters 30–32, Ellen White covers the raising of children in four stages. First, she focuses on the role of the parents before the child is conceived. The character parents have developed long before the appearance of children has a powerful effect on the child. Second, during the pre-natal period the mother's behavior and the father's treatment of the mother is critical to the child's physical, mental, and spiritual development. Third, she focuses on the training and nurture that must take place in the early years of development. Finally, she focuses on the impact of the choices young people make when they reach the teen years. This chapter focuses particularly on stages three and four.

The stories of Samson and John the Baptist are biblical examples of the importance of child training. Parents need to understand the principles of child training and the laws of nature relating to it.

The more quiet and simple the life of the infant, the better. Babies should be kept free from every influence that would tend to weaken or poison the system. Considerable space is given to how infants should be dressed, how the temperature of the room they are in should be regulated, and the importance of lots of fresh air. When properly dressed, children should spend much time in the open air.

While a quiet and simple life for children is important, it is not incompatible with the best kind of stimulation: travel, quality concerts, gardens and zoos, museums, or hiking and biking through dramatic natural settings (among other things).

The best food for infants is that which nature has provided, breast feeding. But Ellen White does not limit the value of breast-feeding to nutrition, she also sees emotional and character implications.

As children grow out of babyhood, they need to be taught good dietary habits: regularity, moderation, and wholesome choices. It is equally important for mealtimes to be a happy, cheerful time. But children's preferences in these matters should also be respected.

Parents are also encouraged to study the causes of the illnesses that their children contract and correct those causes. Related to this is the importance of a practical knowledge of physiology. The advice in these last paragraphs is connected with an important theological statement: "It is not a 'mysterious providence' that removes the little children. God does not desire their death." God is often blamed when children die prematurely. But it is not God who "took them," such deaths are a consequence of human decisions and the actions of the great enemy in the cosmic conflict.

QUOTABLE QUOTES

"Every influence that affects the health of the body has its bearing upon mind and character. Too much importance cannot be placed upon the early training of children. The lessons learned, the habits formed, during the years of infancy and childhood, have more to do with the formation of the character and the direction of the life than have all the instruction and training of after years."

"Most of the evils that are bringing misery and ruin to the race might be prevented, and the power to deal with them rests to a great degree with parents. It is not a 'mysterious providence' that removes the little children. God does not desire their death."

"The more quiet and simple the life of the child, the more favorable it will be to both physical and mental development. At all times the mother should endeavor to be quiet, calm, and self-possessed. Many infants are extremely susceptible to nervous excitement, and the mother's gentle, unhurried manner will have a soothing influence that will be of untold benefit to the child."

THE MORE QUIET AND SIMPLE THE LIFE OF THE INFANT, THE BETTER.

"Parents should train the appetites of their children and should not permit the use of unwholesome foods. But in the effort to regulate the diet, we should be careful not to err in requiring children to eat that which is distasteful, or to eat more than is needed. Children have rights, they have preferences, and when these preferences are reasonable they should be respected."

"Teach your children from the cradle to practice self-denial and self-control. Teach them to enjoy the beauties of nature and in useful employments to exercise systematically all the powers of body and mind. Bring them up to have sound constitutions and good morals, to have sunny dispositions and sweet tempers. Impress upon their tender minds the truth that God does not design that we should live for present gratification merely, but for our ultimate good."

"Above all things else, let parents surround their children with an atmosphere of cheerfulness, courtesy, and love. A home where love dwells, and where it is expressed in looks, in words, and in acts, is a place where angels delight to manifest their presence."

"Parents, let the sunshine of love, cheerfulness, and happy contentment enter your own hearts, and let its sweet, cheering influence pervade your home. . . . The atmosphere thus created will be to the children what air and sunshine are to the vegetable world, promoting health and vigor of mind and body."

@TWEETS_OF_HEALING

When it comes 2 the #child's physical well-being, nothng is unimportant.

#Parents should understand the principles that underlie the care & training of #children.

#Parents should study the laws of #nature. 2 assume the responsibilities of #parenthood wtout such preparation is a #sin.

Most of the #evils that r bringing misery & ruin 2 the race might b prevented.

The more quiet & simple the #life of the #child, the more favorable it will b 2 both physical & mental development.

Every influence that affects the #health of the #body has its bearing upon mind & character.

It is not a 'mysterious providence' that ends the #lives of little #children. @God does not desire their #death.

The #baby should b kept free frm every influence that would tend 2 weaken or 2 #poison the system.

The 1 who nurses a #baby imparts her own temper & temperament 2 the #child.

Little ones need 2 learn that they #eat 2 live, not #live 2 eat.

We should not require that #children #eat that which is distasteful 2 them, or 2 eat more than is needed.

Teach ur #children frm the cradle 2 practice self-denial & self-control.

Above all else, let #parents surround their #children wt an atmosphere of cheerfulness, courtesy & #love.

DISCUSSION QUESTIONS

1. This chapter strongly affirms that the more quiet and simple the life of the child, the better. How do you actually carry that out in a noisy and distracting world?
2. Ellen White affirms breast-feeding as not only nutritious, but offering important emotional and character implications. To what degree have these latter insights been affirmed by recent scientific discoveries?

HOME INFLUENCES

CH. 33, PP. 388-394

SUMMARY

The focus of this chapter is on the "atmosphere" of the family. It can be a place of cheerfulness, courtesy, love, happiness, and peace.

THOUGHTS

While the mother is again the focus of this chapter, there is considerable focus also on the father and how the relationship of mother and father affects the atmosphere of the home.

Young children need companionship and rarely can enjoy themselves alone. The mother, therefore, needs to spend a great deal of time with them, enter into their feelings, and direct their amusements and employments. By patient, watchful love she can turn their minds in the right direction and guard them against becoming dependent and self-absorbed. If children don't find companionship in the family, they will look elsewhere for it, and mind and character may be endangered there.

Mothers must avoid becoming so busy with home duties (particularly extra sewing in pursuit of fashion) that they handle the children in an arbitrary fashion and don't give them the companionship, even-handedness, and direction they need.

The father is to be the law-maker of the household, enforcing the sterner virtues of energy, courage, diligence, and practical usefulness, with an eye to God's Word (such a sentence can be abused, so explore with caution). But

THE RELATIONSHIP BETWEEN HUSBAND AND WIFE IS ALSO CRITICAL TO HOW THE CHILDREN TURN OUT.

he must avoid discouraging the children. He is to combine affection with authority and sympathy with firmness and restraint. He is to particularly cultivate friendship with his son. And no matter how stressful employment becomes, he is to always enter the home with smiles and pleasant words. He is also the priest of the family, who leads in family worship. Strict distinction of parenting roles was part of the culture in the Victorian era. Some of this language comes across in an uncomfortable way in today's world, but the idea of parents playing "good cop/bad cop" roles does connect today, although maybe not so strongly gender related as expressed here. Today women are expected to be more assertive and men more nurturing than was the case in the late nineteenth century.

The relationship between husband and wife is also critical to how the children turn out. At the root of parental guidance is gaining the victory over self. That includes studying each other's happiness and never failing in the small courtesies that brighten the life. They should be united in their child raising and not make the work more difficult for each other. The children need to see that the parents love them and will do all in their power to make each other and the children happy. Parenting is challenging under the best of circumstances and parents need all the encouragement they can get.

Under the wise and loving guidance of a true home, evil and other companionships will not attract the children.

At least three realities of today's home are not addressed in this counsel and make it difficult to carry out. First, it does not address a home in which the mother is often gone in pursuit of income or the mission of the church (though Ellen White's home was exactly like that, she does not offer that kind of home as an option). And it also does not address a home with media options such as television and the Internet. And today mothers spend next to no time at all in the making of clothes, a major issue in the chapter and related ones. How does the counsel of this chapter apply to today's home?

Science today strongly supports the importance of structure and calm in the lives of children, particularly those with ADD or autism.

Something not expressed in this chapter, but consistent with Ellen

White's counsel elsewhere, is that in situations where parents are uncertain as to the best course of action toward children, it is best to err on the side of mercy, love, cheerfulness, and courtesy rather than authority, firmness, and restraint (where one has to choose).

QUOTABLE QUOTES

"The home should be to the children the most attractive place in the world, and the mother's presence should be its greatest attraction. Children have sensitive, loving natures. They are easily pleased and easily made unhappy. By gentle discipline, in loving words and acts, mothers may bind their children to their hearts."

"The father should enforce in his family the sterner virtues—energy, integrity, honesty, patience, courage, diligence, and practical usefulness. And what he requires of his children he himself should practice, illustrating these virtues in his own manly bearing."

"In a sense the father is the priest of the household, laying upon the family altar the morning and evening sacrifice. But the wife and children should unite in prayer and join in the song of praise. In the morning before he leaves home for his daily labor, let the father gather his children about him and, bowing before God, commit them to the care of the Father in heaven. When the cares of the day are past, let the family unite in offering grateful prayer and raising the song of praise, in acknowledgment of divine care during the day."

"Home should be a place where cheerfulness, courtesy, and love abide; and where these graces dwell, there will abide happiness and peace. Troubles may invade, but these are the lot of humanity. Let patience, gratitude, and love keep sunshine in the heart, though the day may be ever so cloudy. In such homes angels of God abide."

"Parents, let your children see that you love them and will do all in your power to make them happy. If you do so, your necessary restrictions will have far greater weight in their young minds."

"Brought up under the wise and loving guidance of a true home, children will have no desire to wander away in search of pleasure and companionship. Evil will not attract them. The spirit that prevails in the home will mold their characters; they will form habits and principles that will be a strong defense against temptation when they shall leave the home shelter and take their place in the world."

@TWEETS_OF_HEALING

The #home should b 2 the #children the most attractive place in the #world.

If #children don't find companionship in the #family, they will look elsewhere for it.

What the #father requires of his #children, he should himself practice.

Regardless of business perplexities, the #father should enter his #home wt smiles & pleasant words.

Let the #husband & #wife study each other's #happiness, nvr failing in the small courtesies & kindly acts.

Where cheerfulness, courtesy & #love abide thr will b #happiness & peace.

At the root of parental guidance is gaining the victory over #self.

#Parents should b united in their #child raising & not make the wrk more difficult for each other.

#Parents, let ur #children see that u #love them & will do all in ur power 2 make them #happy.

DISCUSSION QUESTIONS

1. This chapter does not address a home where both parents are away at work, where the home contains influences such as television and the Internet, or where mothers spend very little time in the making and mending of clothes. How does the counsel of this chapter apply to so many homes today?
2. When Ellen White says that by gentle discipline mothers may bind their children to their hearts (page 388), what does she mean? How do you actually do that in practice?

TRUE **EDUCATION**, A MISSIONARY **TRAINING**

CH. 34, PP. 395–406

SUMMARY

True education is training for missionary work, which Ellen White defines as to be representatives of God, to reveal His Spirit, to manifest His character, and to do His work of service in the world. One can be a missionary in common tasks in one's homeland as well as pioneering far from home.

THOUGHTS

This chapter is part of a series on parenting and child training principles. Although not directly stated, the focus in this chapter seems to be on the age of responsibility (roughly the teen years, perhaps through high school).

True education prepares people for missionary work. Such work can be performed in the circle of the home, in common vocations, as teachers of the gospel, and also in heathen lands.

Youth stand at a parting of the ways. Whether their lives are a blessing or a curse is often decided in the teen years. The job of parents is not to repress youthful activity but to guide it in the right direction. We need to surround them with the kinds of influences that will cause them to choose a life of service rather than self-indulgence. Life is full of opportunity, but once lost, those opportunities are often gone forever.

The ideal is for youth to excel in all things that are unselfish, high, and noble. Christ is the pattern. So education needs to engage the whole person

TRUE EDUCATION PREPARES PEOPLE FOR MISSIONARY WORK.

with the highest science being that of saving souls. True education directs the attention away from money, fame, and power to things of true worth.

Two important principles of education are (1) learning by imparting and (2) guarding the youthful associations to preserve them from harmful companionships. The latter principle is supported by Bible texts such as John 17:14; Romans 12:2; and 2 Corinthians 6:14–18. Rightly handled, godly education can mold the entire fabric of society.

Family life has changed a great deal in the last hundred years. In many ways, the implementation of the above is much more difficult than when Ellen White wrote, and also more needed. Were she alive today, it is likely she would advise parents to limit exposure to media as a main source of outside influences, even when the children are home-schooled.

QUOTABLE QUOTES

"True education is missionary training. Every son and daughter of God is called to be a missionary; we are called to the service of God and our fellow men; and to fit us for this service should be the object of our education."

"Let the youth be impressed with the thought that they are not their own. They belong to Christ. They are the purchase of His blood, the claim of His love. They live because He keeps them by His power. Their time, their strength, their capabilities are His, to be developed, to be trained, to be used for Him."

"Life is mysterious and sacred. It is the manifestation of God Himself, the source of all life. Precious are its opportunities, and earnestly should they be improved. Once lost, they are gone forever."

"God looks into the tiny seed that He Himself has formed, and sees wrapped within it the beautiful flower, the shrub, or the lofty, wide-spreading tree. So does He see the possibilities in every human being. We are here for a purpose. God has given us His plan for our life, and He desires us to reach the highest standard of development."

"It should be their (youth) ambition to excel in all things that are unselfish, high, and noble. Let them look to Christ as the pattern after which they are to be fashioned. The holy ambition that He revealed in His life they are to cherish—an ambition to make the world better for their having lived in it. This is the work to which they are called."

"Education is not complete unless the body, the mind, and the heart are equally educated. The character must receive proper discipline for its fullest and highest development. All the faculties of mind and body are to be developed and rightly trained. It is a duty to cultivate and to exercise every power that will render us more efficient workers for God."

"With the people of that age the value of things was estimated by outward show. As religion had declined in power, it had increased in pomp. The educators of the time sought to command respect by display and ostentation. To all this the life of Jesus presented a marked contrast. His life demonstrated the worthlessness of those things that men regarded as life's great essentials."

"Every child and every youth should have a knowledge of himself. He should understand the physical habitation that God has given him, and the laws by which it is kept in health. All should be thoroughly grounded in the common branches of education. And they should have industrial training that will make them men and women of practical ability, fitted for the duties of everyday life. To this should be added training and practical experience in various lines of missionary effort."

"As youth learn, let them impart their knowledge. It is thus that their minds will acquire discipline and power. It is the use they make of knowledge that determines the value of their education. To spend a long time in study, with no effort to impart what is gained, often proves a hindrance rather than a help to real development."

"Throughout the world, society is in disorder, and a thorough transformation is needed. The education given to the youth is to mold the whole social fabric."

@TWEETS_OF_HEALING

Every son & daughter of @God is called 2 b a #missionary.

Whether ppl's #lives r a blessing or a curse is often decided in the teen years.

#Life is full of opportunity, bt once lost those opportunities r often gone forever.

#Education is not complete unless the #body, the mind & the heart r equally educated.

True #education includes the whole being.

True #education directs the attention away frm money, fame & power 2 things of true worth.

Every #child & every youth should hve a #knowledge of himself.

It is not until they teach what they hve learned that youthful minds acquire discipline & power.

The #education given 2 youth molds the entire fabric of society.

DISCUSSION QUESTIONS

1. When Ellen White describes true education as that which directs the attention away from money, fame, and power to things of true worth (pages 398–402), what is she talking about? How do you actually do that?
2. Ellen White says that "education is not complete unless the body, the mind, and the heart are equally educated." Where is that happening in Adventist education today? How can we draw nearer to that ideal?

A TRUE KNOWLEDGE OF GOD

CH. 35, PP. 409–429

SUMMARY

Our knowledge of God is partial and imperfect, yet a true knowledge of God is essential to true education and character development. While God can be experienced through the works of His creation, the clearest revelation of God is found in Jesus Christ, especially at the Cross.

THOUGHTS

Although not directly stated, the focus of this chapter seems most appropriate to college-level education.

A true knowledge of God is the foundation of all true education and service. It is the essential preparation both for this life and for the life to come. We are to become like Him in character and then by a life of service reveal Him to the world. But in order to become like Him, we need to know what He is like.

Through nature, marred though it is, we receive glimpses of God's goodness and His love of beauty. Nature itself is not God, but it testifies to His character and power. Above all else in creation, humanity was intended to express God's thoughts and reveal His glory.

Although all knowledge of God is partial and imperfect, the greatest revelation of God is to be found in Jesus Christ. God's personality and character are most clearly revealed there. At the Cross, the revelation of God's love to human beings is made known.

This chapter offers strong encouragement to learn all you can in as many fields as possible, in other words, get a broad education. There is strong support here for the study of science and the appreciation of beauty in all of its God-given forms. Not only so, the chapter makes the strong point that every legitimate job is sacred and every field of learning is potentially sacred.

The chapter also highlights the two main sources of knowledge, nature and Scripture, or as they are called by scholars, general and special revelation. There is much about God that can be learned from nature, but there are also limitations in that knowledge that are filled in by Scripture. In the words of Niebuhr, as paraphrased to us by Richard Rice, "Special revelation completes the incompleteness, clarifies the obscurities, and corrects the falsifications of general revelation."

A reading knowledge of Ellen White highlights the importance of a right knowledge of God and of God's character. In order to become like God, we must know Him aright.

QUOTABLE QUOTES

"We are here to become like God in character, and by a life of service to reveal Him to the world. In order to be co-workers with God, in order to become like Him and to reveal His character, we must know Him aright."

"A knowledge of God is the foundation of all true education and of all true service. It is the only real safeguard against temptation. It is this alone that can make us like God in character. This is the knowledge needed by all who are working for the uplifting of their fellow men. Transformation of character, purity of life, efficiency in service, adherence to correct principles, all depend upon a right knowledge of God. This knowledge is the essential preparation both for this life and for the life to come."

"The things of nature that we now behold give us but a faint conception of Eden's glory. Sin has marred earth's beauty; on all things may be seen traces of the work of evil. Yet much that is beautiful remains. Nature testifies that One infinite in power, great in goodness, mercy, and love, created the earth, and filled it with life and gladness. Even in their blighted state, all things reveal the handiwork of the great Master Artist. Wherever we turn, we may hear the voice of God, and see evidences of His goodness."

"God's handiwork in nature is not God Himself in nature. The things of nature are an expression of God's character and power; but we are not to regard nature as God. The artistic skill of human beings produces very beautiful workmanship, things that delight the eye, and these things reveal to us something of the thought of the designer; but the thing made is not the maker. It is not the work, but the workman, that is counted worthy of honor. So while nature is an expression of God's thought, it is not nature, but the God of nature, that is to be exalted."

EVERY LEGITIMATE JOB IS SACRED AND EVERY FIELD OF LEARNING IS POTENTIALLY SACRED.

"Above all lower orders of being, God designed that man, the crowning work of His creation, should express His thought and reveal His glory. But man is not to exalt himself as God."

"In the heavens above, in the earth, in the broad waters of the ocean, we see the handiwork of God. All created things testify to His power, His wisdom, His love. Yet not from the stars or the ocean or the cataract can we learn of the personality of God as it was revealed in Christ. God saw that a clearer revelation than nature was needed to portray both His personality and His character. He sent His Son into the world to manifest, so far as could be endured by human sight, the nature and the attributes of the invisible God."

@TWEETS_OF_HEALING

In order 2 bcome like #Him & 2 reveal #His #character, we must know Him aright.

A #knowledge of @God is the foundation of all true #education & of all true #service.

A right #knowledge of @God is the essential preparation both for this #life & for the life 2 come.

The things of #nature that we now behold give us bt a faint conception of Eden's #glory.

He who placed the #pearls in the ocean & the amethyst & chrysolite among the rocks, is a lover of the beautiful.

The things of #nature r an expression of @God's character & power; bt we r not 2 regard nature as @God.

The wrk of #creation cn not b explained by #science.

The stars, the ocean, or the cataract cn not teach us the #personality of @God as it was revealed in @Christ.

Our #knowledge of @God is partial & imperfect.

DISCUSSION QUESTIONS

1. When Ellen White writes that "we are to become like God in character," what is she talking about?
   - Note: the role of "service."

Read: *"The work of creation cannot be explained by science. What science can explain the mystery of life?"*

2. Do you agree or disagree with the above quote?

DANGER IN SPECULATIVE KNOWLEDGE

CH. 36, PP. 427–438

SUMMARY

Reason should certainly be used to plumb the depths of human experience, but when it comes to a knowledge of God, reason needs to know its limits.

THOUGHTS

In many ways, the title is more negative than the tone of the chapter, perhaps reflecting the conflicted times in which it was written (see below). An alternative title for the chapter could have been "Theology as Doxology (Song of Praise)."

In the quest for human knowledge, there is a danger of exalting human reasoning above its true value and proper sphere. When it comes to God, the clearest knowledge comes from revelation rather than reason. And that knowledge does not bring us under the control of Satan.

One of the most dangerous theories about God is the idea that God is an essence that not only pervades all of nature but is equivalent to it (commonly called pantheism). If God and nature are essentially the same, then the solution to human problems comes from within rather than from without, as the Scriptures teach. Pantheism does away with the necessity for the atonement and undermines the message of Scripture. Human power without God is worthless.

The context of this part of the chapter is the Kellogg crisis around the

HUMAN POWER WITHOUT GOD IS WORTHLESS.

turn of the century in Adventist history. Pantheism is the belief that God and the universe are identical. It denies the transcendence and personality of God. Pantheism can sound biblical in the sense that God permeates all things. The difference is that in the biblical view, God is not limited to the creation; He both fills and transcends nature. Many doubt that Kellogg was a pantheist in the classical sense; he comes closer to what some have called Panentheism ("God is in everything"). In the biblical view, God fills all nature, but is distinct from it. He created nature out of nothing. Nature is a gift from God, not a "given" in its own right. Kellogg emphasized the presence of God in all things but blurred the distinctions between God and nature.

When it comes to God, we are as ignorant as little children, but through revelation our understanding is sufficient to love and obey Him. The mysteries of God's being are not found by scientific research but by humbly receiving the revelation of Scripture and conforming the life to the will of God. God's greatness is spelled out by such texts as Isaiah 6:1–7; 40:12–28; Psalms 139:1–6; 145:3–21; Romans 11:34–36; and Job 37:5–24. Biblical stories such as the Israelites who ventured to open the ark, Uzzah, the burning bush, Jacob's ladder, and the high priest's cautious entry into the Most Holy Place all illustrate the reverence and humility we ought to exhibit as we approach the subject of God.

Genuine scholarship is compatible with the concerns of this chapter. The greatness of a scholar consists not in how much he or she knows, but rather in the knowledge of how little he or she knows. Those who know the least are often the most confident in their "knowledge." True scholars are genuinely humble.

In this context, it is helpful to remind ourselves of Ellen White's clearest statement on the nature of God:

"The mighty power that works through all nature and sustains all things is not, as some men of science represent, merely an all-pervading principle, an actuating energy. God is a spirit; yet He is a personal being, for man was made in His image.

"God's handiwork in nature is not God Himself in nature. The things of nature are an expression of God's character; by them we may understand His love, His power, and His glory; but we are not to regard nature as God.

The artistic skill of human beings produces very beautiful workmanship, things that delight the eye and these things give us something of the idea of the designer; but the thing made is not the man. It is not the work, but the workman, that is counted worthy of honor. So, while nature is an expression of God's thought, it is not nature but the God of nature that is to be exalted" (*Testimonies for the Church,* 8:263).

QUOTABLE QUOTES

"One of the greatest evils that attends the quest for knowledge, the investigations of science, is the disposition to exalt human reasoning above its true value and its proper sphere. Many attempt to judge of the Creator and His works by their own imperfect knowledge of science."

"Our condition through sin is unnatural, and the power that restores us must be supernatural, else it has no value. There is but one power that can break the hold of evil from the hearts of men, and that is the power of God in Jesus Christ."

"The revelation of Himself that God has given in His word is for our study. This we may seek to understand. But beyond this we are not to penetrate. The highest intellect may tax itself until it is wearied out in conjectures regarding the nature of God, but the effort will be fruitless. This problem has not been given us to solve. No human mind can comprehend God. None are to indulge in speculation regarding His nature. Here silence is eloquence. The Omniscient One is above discussion."

"We are as ignorant of God as little children; but, as little children, we may love and obey Him."

"Neither by searching the recesses of the earth nor in vain endeavors to penetrate the mysteries of God's being, is wisdom found. It is found, rather, in humbly receiving the revelation that He has been pleased to give, and in conforming the life to His will."

"Skeptics refuse to believe in God because they cannot comprehend the infinite power by which He reveals Himself. But God is to be acknowledged as much from what He does not reveal of Himself, as from that which is open to our limited comprehension. Both in divine revelation and in nature, God has given mysteries to command our faith. This must be so. We may be ever searching, ever inquiring, ever learning, and yet there is an infinity beyond."

"Let none seek with presumptuous hand to lift the veil that conceals His glory. 'Unsearchable are His judgments, and His ways past finding out.' Romans 11:33. It is a proof of His mercy that there is the hiding of His power; for to lift the veil that conceals the divine presence is death. No mortal mind can penetrate the secrecy in which the Mighty One dwells and works. Only that which He sees fit to reveal can we comprehend of Him."

@TWEETS_OF_HEALING

Our condition thru #sin is unnatural & the power that restores us must b supernatural, else it has no #value.

The revelation of #Himself that @God has given us in #His #Word is for our #study.

We r as ignorant of @God as little #children, but, as little children, we may #love & obey #Him.

Wisdom is found in humbly receiving the revelation that @God has been please 2 give & in conforming the #life 2 #His will.

Only that which @God sees fit 2 reveal cn we comprehend of #Him.

DISCUSSION QUESTIONS

1. What is the role of faith in science and religion? Is there a "faith element" in both of those philosophies and their understanding in the world?

   Note this quote: *"Divine inspiration asks many questions which the most profound scholar cannot answer. These questions were not asked that we might answer them, but to call our attention to the deep mysteries of god and to teach us that our wisdom is limited; that in the surroundings of our daily life there are many things beyond the comprehension of finite beings."*

2. Why "mysteries"?

THE FALSE AND THE TRUE IN EDUCATION

CH. 37, PP. 439-450

SUMMARY

The chapter contrasts two kinds of education: (1) a knowledge of earthly things that does not acknowledge God, and (2) a wisdom regarding heavenly things that puts God and eternity first in life. The ideal is a wisdom that combines a knowledge of earthly things with a full commitment to God and eternity.

THOUGHTS

Read in isolation, this chapter can be somewhat disturbing, as it seems at times to disparage science and reason, or even higher education as a whole, things that are strongly encouraged in their right place elsewhere in Ellen White's writings (see, for example, her remarkable endorsement of seeking education at secular institutions in *Testimonies for the Church,* 5:583, 584). This chapter may reflect anti-intellectual trends that were common from time to time during her life. One possibility is that the original writing upon which this chapter is based occurred in the context of the Battle Creek debacle in the early to mid-1870s. At that time attempts were made to cut the spiritual and the work-study components completely out of the curriculum. She was not pleased!

Ellen White must always be understood in context. One way to provide that context is to read this chapter together with the next (chap. 38: "The Importance of Seeking True Knowledge"). The emphasis in this chapter is more on the false; the next chapter focuses on true education. Together,

THERE IS A FORM OF EDUCATION THAT PRODUCES SKEPTICS RATHER THAN BELIEVERS.

they provide a balance that might be missing with this chapter alone. Chapter 35 ("A True Knowledge of God") also provides a positive balance to the more negative message of this chapter, as does the statement toward the end of this chapter: "It is right for the youth to feel that they must reach the highest development of their mental powers. We would not restrict the education to which God has set no limit. But our attainments avail nothing if not put to use for the honor of God and the good of humanity" (page 449).

There is a form of education that produces skeptics rather than believers. The natural inclination of human nature toward evil makes the choice of education all the more critical. Skepticism is attractive to the human mind, particularly young minds. And as faith in God is weakened, so the ability to resist temptation is weakened. What is needed are schools where students are taught that true greatness is found in honoring God and revealing His character in daily life.

Why are there so many true, helpful, and powerful things in secular education? Ellen White's answer is that Satan himself was educated in the heavenly courts and knows good as well as evil. But the mingling of the two can be very deceptive.

Among the lines of learning where there is a mingling of good and evil, Ellen White includes positive works by infidel authors, much historical and theological study (if its focus is on intellect rather than heart, pride of attainment rather than humility before God, speculation rather than biblical truth), the great classics of antiquity, current sensational fiction, myths, and fairy tales. While it is true that higher learning can produce pride, it can also produce humility, as a person discovers how vast their ignorance truly is.

True education focuses not so much on the learning of facts and concepts as on knowledge that can be utilized. Heart education is far more important than book learning. True education builds humility rather than pride. It directs the attention to eternal things rather than the temporary. True education helps youth understand their weakness so they will turn to God for strength.

It may be helpful to make a distinction or two here. Ellen White is not against good theories, she is against "mere" theorizing. In other words, theories are useful when integrated with practice. Theories that guide and motivate good practices are useful.

QUOTABLE QUOTES

"The mastermind in the confederacy of evil is ever working to keep out of sight the words of God, and to bring into view the opinions of men. He means that we shall not hear the voice of God, saying, 'This is the way, walk ye in it.' Isaiah 30:21."

"Philosophical speculation and scientific research in which God is not acknowledged are making skeptics of thousands. In the schools of today the conclusions that learned men have reached as the result of their scientific investigations are carefully taught and fully explained; while the impression is distinctly given that if these learned men are correct, the Bible cannot be. Skepticism is attractive to the human mind. The youth see in it an independence that captivates the imagination, and they are deceived. Satan triumphs. He nourishes every seed of doubt that is sown in young hearts. He causes it to grow and bear fruit, and soon a plentiful harvest of infidelity is reaped."

"It is because the human heart is inclined to evil that it is so dangerous to sow the seeds of skepticism in young minds. Whatever weakens faith in God robs the soul of power to resist temptation. It removes the only real safeguard against sin. We are in need of schools where the youth shall be taught that greatness consists in honoring God by revealing His character in daily life. Through His word and His works we need to learn of God, that our lives may fulfill His purpose."

"(The study of sacred history) will give broad, comprehensive views of life. It will help us to understand something of its relations and dependencies, how wonderfully we are bound together in the great brotherhood of society and nations, and to how great an extent the oppression and degradation of one member means loss to all. But history, as commonly studied, is concerned with man's achievements, his victories in battle, his success in attaining power and greatness. God's agency in the affairs of men is lost sight of. Few study the working out of His purpose in the rise and fall of nations."

"Your intellectual pride will not aid you in communicating with souls that are perishing for want of the bread of life. In your study of these books you are allowing them to take the place of the practical lessons you should be learning from Christ. With the results of this study the people are not fed. Very little of the research which is so wearying to the mind furnishes that which will help one to be a successful laborer for souls."

"That which I have seen of eternal things, and that which I have seen of the weakness of humanity, has deeply impressed my mind and influenced my lifework. I see nothing wherein man should be praised or glorified. I see no reason why the opinions of worldly-wise men and so-called great men should be trusted in and exalted."

"It is right for the youth to feel that they must reach the highest development of their mental powers. We would not restrict the education to which God has set no limit. But our attainments avail nothing if not put to use for the honor of God and the good of humanity. It is not well to crowd the mind with studies that require intense application, but that are not brought into use in practical life. Such education will be a loss to the student. For these studies lessen his desire and inclination for the studies that would fit him for usefulness and enable him to fulfill his responsibilities."

@TWEETS_OF_HEALING

@Satan is ever wrking 2 keep out of sight the words of @God & 2 bring into view the opinions of #men.

Philosophical speculation & #scientific research in which @God is not acknowledged r making skeptics of thousands.

Whatever weakens #faith in @God robs the #soul of power 2 resist #temptation.

We need schools where the youth r taught that gr8ness consists in honoring @God by revealing #His #character in daily #life.

A practical training is worth more than any amount of mere #theorizing.

If the youth understood their own #weakness, they would find in @God their #strength.

DISCUSSION QUESTIONS

SMALL GROUPS Discussion:
General observation: **Ellen White comes across as if she is against reading other books, but the *Bible only*—and that constitutes "*true education.*"**

1. How far should we take the point of reading other books, (classics/fiction), or what Ellen White calls "infidel authors"? Is reading of ALL such literature wrong? Is there a PRINCIPLE? What may be some of the dangers that Ellen White is talking about?

- NOTE: Examples of Bible fiction(s):
  - o see Luke 16—the rich man and Lazarus
  - o Parables . . .

Ellen White's use of fiction:

- o see *Testimonies for the Church,* 2:594–597.
- o *Sabbath Readings for the Home Circle* (many of the stories are fictional)
- o Recommended John Bunyan's *Pilgrim's Progress* (see *The Great Controversy,* 252). She called it a "wonderful allegory."

Read: *"Philosophical speculation and scientific research in which God is not acknowledged are making skeptics of thousands."*

2. Is that true for studying medicine? How and why?

THE IMPORTANCE OF SEEKING TRUE KNOWLEDGE

CH. 38, PP. 451-457

SUMMARY

The highest possible knowledge is the revelation of God and Jesus Christ as expressed in character. The emphasis in this chapter is on steady, lifelong commitment to God and the spiritual growth that results from such commitment.

THOUGHTS

According to this chapter, spiritual life is hard work, it is lifelong, it is self-denying and self-renouncing, it is like a warfare that requires training and discipline, it requires intense focus, and it must be God-directed at all times. When engaged in in these ways, the result is an ever-growing knowledge of God and spiritual commitment that results in greater service.

Reading this chapter can be a depressing experience for those who struggle with self-discipline. The chapter is strong on exhortation but seems almost void of encouraging words. Unfortunately, the more we concentrate on sanctification (spiritual growth and self-control), the more miserable we may become. So the reading of this chapter needs to be balanced with the uplifting readings in the last four chapters. There is also a powerful balancing statement in *Steps to Christ,* page 64: "There are those who have known the pardoning love of Christ and who really desire to be children of God, yet they realize that their character is imperfect, their life faulty, and they are ready to doubt whether their hearts have been renewed by the Holy Spirit. To such I would say, Do not draw back in despair. We shall often have to bow down and weep at the feet of Jesus because of our shortcomings and mistakes, but we are not to be discouraged. Even if we are overcome by the enemy, we are not cast off, not forsaken and rejected of God."

The knowledge that is talked about in this chapter is not intellectual knowledge. It is knowledge as related to character. It provides a true knowledge of self. One of the most difficult things human beings face is how to change our habits in a positive way. The true knowledge sought in this chapter is knowledge of how to turn our thoughts away from self and toward God. In the context of a secure relationship with a loving God, the counsels in this chapter can encourage a closer and closer walk with God.

QUOTABLE QUOTES

"Wrongs cannot be righted, nor can reformations in conduct be made by a few feeble, intermittent efforts. Character building is the work, not of a day, nor of a year, but of a lifetime. The struggle for conquest over self, for holiness and heaven, is a lifelong struggle. Without continual effort and constant activity, there can be no advancement in the divine life, no attainment of the victor's crown."

"The life of the apostle Paul was a constant conflict with self. He said, "I die daily." 1 Corinthians 15:31. His will and his desires every day conflicted with duty and the will of God. Instead of following inclination, he did God's will, however crucifying to his nature.

"There is a science of Christianity to be mastered—a science as much deeper, broader, higher than any human science as the heavens are higher than the earth. The mind is to be disciplined, educated, trained; for we are to do service for God in ways that are not in harmony with inborn inclination. Hereditary and cultivated tendencies to evil must be overcome. Often the education and training of a lifetime must be discarded, that one may become a learner in the school of Christ. Our hearts must be educated to become steadfast in God. We are to form habits of thought that will enable us to resist temptation. We must learn to look upward."

"The thoughts must be centered upon God. We must put forth earnest effort to overcome the evil tendencies of the natural heart. Our efforts, our self-denial and perseverance, must be proportionate to the infinite value of the object of which we are in pursuit. Only by overcoming as Christ overcame shall we win the crown of life."

"In order to receive help from Christ, we must realize our need. We must have a true knowledge of ourselves. It is only he who knows himself to be a sinner that Christ can save. Only as we see our utter helplessness and renounce all self-trust, shall we lay hold on divine power.

"It is not only at the beginning of the Christian life that this renunciation of self is to be made. At every advance step heavenward it is to be renewed. All our good works are dependent on a power outside of ourselves; therefore there needs to be a continual reaching out of the heart after God, a constant, earnest confession of sin and humbling of the soul before Him. Perils surround us; and we are safe only as we feel our weakness and cling with the grasp of faith to our mighty Deliverer."

"We must turn away from a thousand topics that invite attention. There are matters that consume time and arouse inquiry, but end in nothing. The highest interests demand the close attention and energy that are so often given to comparatively insignificant things."

"The knowledge of God and of Jesus Christ expressed in character is an exaltation above everything else that is esteemed on earth or in heaven. It is the very highest education. It is the key that opens the portals of the heavenly city. This knowledge it is God's purpose that all who put on Christ shall possess."

@TWEETS_OF_HEALING

As the sacrifice in our behalf was complete, so our restoration frm the defilement of sin is 2 b complete.

#Character building is the wrk, not of a day, nor of a year, bt of a #lifetime.

The #life of the apostle Paul was in constant conflict wt #self.

The mind is 2 b disciplined & trained; for we must at times serve @God in ways that r not natural 2 us.

The angels of @God r seeking 2 attract us frm ourselves & frm earthly things. Let them not labor in vain.

The #thoughts must b #centered on @God.

Only as we see our utter helplessness & renounce all self-trust, shall we lay hold on divine #power.

Perils surround us; & we r safe only as we feel our weakness & cling wt the grasp of #faith 2 our mighty #Deliverer.

We must turn away frm a thousand topics that invite attention.

The #knowledge of @God expressed in character exalts 1 above any other quality.

DISCUSSION QUESTIONS

1. Discuss: What is "truth"? Is it relative? Is it concrete?
2. According to Ellen White in this chapter, how do we come to the knowledge of "truth(s)"? What kind of "truth" is Ellen White talking about?
3. Are Adventist schools and universities justified to demand a "religious class" for its students as part of the curriculum? Why or why not? (How do you see the role of the School of Religion in your education here?)

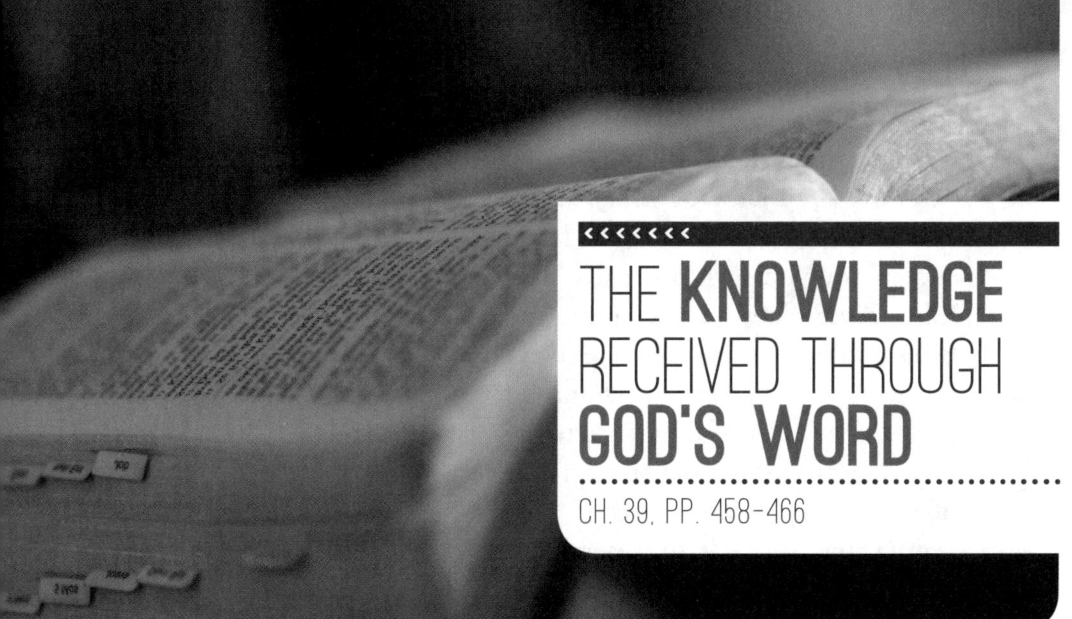

THE **KNOWLEDGE** RECEIVED THROUGH **GOD'S WORD**

CH. 39, PP. 458-466

SUMMARY

Received, believed, and obeyed, the Bible is the great instrumentality in the transformation of character. Sin darkens our minds and dims our perceptions. But as sin is purged from our hearts through the Scriptures, God's presence in our lives opens up both the Bible and the book of nature.

THOUGHTS

Youth are easily led into temptation and sin because they do not study the Bible and meditate upon it as they should. The truths of the Bible would produce inward rectitude and strength of principle that would enable them to resist temptation. The mind that is earthly finds no pleasure in God's Word. The mind renewed by the Holy Spirit finds beauty and light in every page. If youth will make the Bible the food of mind and soul, they would be fortified against temptation.

Unless the above principles are in place, those studying the sciences will tend to put nature above God. A correct understanding of both the Bible and science will prove them to be in harmony.

When we read a chapter like this, we need to keep two contexts in mind. First, what did Ellen White actually mean when she wrote these statements back in her time and place? And second, what impact will her choice of words have in today's context? After a hundred years the same words can have very different meanings in another time and place.

YOUTH ARE EASILY LED INTO TEMPTATION AND SIN BECAUSE THEY DO NOT STUDY THE BIBLE AND MEDITATE UPON IT AS THEY SHOULD.

This chapter states what is in some ways the key theme of *The Ministry of Healing,* that the Bible and science illuminate each other. By this, Ellen White does not mean that the Bible and science must line up in every detail, but that an understanding of the Cross and of the character of God are essential to making sense of the results of science. But while stating this principle in general, Ellen White does not explain how (the "hermeneutics") we are to come to such a conclusion. She is casting a vision more than she is explaining how to get there or the exact details one will find when one gets there. In many ways, this is the grounding philosophy behind Loma Linda University and its commitment to the integration of faith and science.

One might get the impression from this statement that the Bible not only comes from God in its spiritual message, but that it is an infallible guide to history, science and even geography. That impression should be balanced with her statements regarding the humanness of Scripture in places such as *Selected Messages,* book 1, pages 19–21 and the introduction to *The Great Controversy.* History tells us that in trying to be true to the Bible, church people have often misread science (Galileo, for example). But we must also be open to the possibility that at times we have misread the Bible as well. So an integration between the two requires rigorous attention to the evidence of both.

One other important insight in the chapter (and also the New Testament) is that the line between the present and eternity is not sharply drawn. Eternity in many ways begins now. The spiritual growth that we experience now and the talents that we train and exercise here will have implications for the kind of life we live in the beyond. The second coming of Jesus is more like a graduation than an awakening into a totally different kind of life.

QUOTABLE QUOTES

"The whole Bible is a revelation of the glory of God in Christ. Received, believed, obeyed, it is the great instrumentality in the transformation of character. It is the grand stimulus, the constraining force, that quickens the physical, mental, and spiritual powers, and directs the life into right channels."

"The reason why the youth, and even those of mature years, are so easily led into temptation and sin, is that they do not study the word of God and meditate upon it as they should. The lack of firm, decided will power, which is manifest in life and character, results from neglect of the sacred instruction of God's word. . . . Few treasure His words in the heart and practice them in the life."

"The mind that is earthly finds no pleasure in contemplating the word of God; but for the mind renewed by the Holy Spirit, divine beauty and celestial light shine from the sacred page."

"Let the youth make the word of God the food of mind and soul. Let the cross of Christ be made the science of all education, the center of all teaching and all study. Let it be brought into the daily experience in practical life. So will the Saviour become to the youth a daily companion and friend."

"Man cannot of himself read aright the teaching of nature. Unless guided by divine wisdom, he exalts nature and the laws of nature above nature's God. This is why mere human ideas in regard to science so often contradict the teaching of God's word. But for those who receive the light of the life of Christ, nature is again illuminated. In the light shining from the cross, we can rightly interpret nature's teaching.

"He who has a knowledge of God and His word through personal experience has a settled faith in the divinity of the Holy Scriptures. . . . To such a student, scientific research will open vast fields of thought and information. As he contemplates the things of nature, a new perception of truth comes to him. The book of nature and the written word shed light upon each other. Both make him better acquainted with God by teaching him of His character and of the laws through which He works."

"Let the student take the Bible as his guide and stand firm for principle, and he may aspire to any height of attainment. All the philosophies of human nature have led to confusion and shame when God has not been recognized as all in all. But the precious faith inspired of God imparts strength and nobility of character. As His goodness, His mercy, and His love are dwelt upon, clearer and still clearer will be the perception of truth; higher, holier, the desire for purity of heart and clearness of thought. The soul dwelling in the pure atmosphere of holy thought is transformed by intercourse with God through the study of His word. Truth is so large, so far-reaching, so deep, so broad, that self is lost sight of. The heart is softened and subdued into humility, kindness, and love. "

"Our lifework here is a preparation for the life eternal. The education begun here will not be completed in this life; it will be going forward through all eternity—ever progressing, never completed. More and more fully will be revealed the wisdom and love of God in the plan of redemption. . . . In the light that shines from the throne, mysteries will disappear, and the soul will be filled with astonishment at the simplicity of the things that were never before comprehended."

@TWEETS_OF_HEALING

Received, believed & obeyed, the #Bible is the gr8 instrumentality in the transformation of #character.

Let the youth make the #word of @God the food of mind & #soul.

Let the #cross of @Christ b made the #science of all #education, the center of all teaching & all study.

The 1 who has a personal exp wt @God & #His #word is prepared 2 engage in the study of #natural #science.

Man cn not of himself read aright the teaching of #nature.

In the #light shining frm the #cross, we cn rightly interpret #nature's teaching.

He who has a #knowledge of @God & His word thru personal exp has a settled faith in the divinity of the #Holy #Scriptures.

It is #sin that darkens our minds & dims our perceptions.

DISCUSSION QUESTIONS

1. What should be the role of the Bible in Christian education in general . . . and in medical education at Loma Linda University, in particular?
    - See the quote: "Let the youth make the word of God the food of mind and soul. Let the cross of Christ be made the science of all education, the center of all teaching and all study. Let it be brought into the daily experience in practical life. So will the Saviour become to the youth a daily companion and friend."

2. How would you interpret the following: "He who has gained a knowledge of God and His word through personal experience is prepared to engage in the study of natural science"? What must be the relationship between the Bible and science in seeking knowledge?

Read: "Now we see through a glass, darkly; but then face to face: now I know in part; but then shall I know even as also I am known" (1 Cor. 13:12, KJV).

3. A true knowledge of God is based on what?
    - Faith
    - Reason

Interesting that we always talk in OPPOSITES:

- Natural vs. supernatural
- Reason vs. revelation
- Science vs. religion
- Law vs. grace
- Body vs. soul
- Secular vs. sacred

Maybe those dichotomies do not exist?

SUMMARY

The main point of this chapter is that spiritual development is about the integration of inner and outer faithfulness to God. God uses trials to foster this integration and prepare people for greater service.

THOUGHTS

Chapters 40–43 are among the most fruitful and inspiring of all of Ellen White's writings. It tells us that the entire goal of Jesus' ministry was to incline the hearts of others toward God. The concept of character is a strong unifying theme throughout chapters 36–43.

To convince others of the grace of God, we need to know its power in our own hearts and lives. The strongest argument in favor of the gospel is a loving and lovable Christian.

God uses trials and obstacles to develop these qualities in us. So it is crucial not to wish for different circumstances but to accept the circumstances in which we find ourselves and apply ourselves to the tasks at hand.

In the future life, we will understand all the seemingly unanswered prayers and disappointed hopes. The life of Moses is a good example.

God esteems people more on the basis of their humility, purity of motive, and beauty of character than on their talents, bustle, and self-importance.

A major theme of this chapter is that God uses suffering to develop beautiful qualities of character in us. These thoughts can be quite encouraging, as finding meaning in suffering helps people to deal with it. But it may be fair to ask the question, Is God's plan for each person as detailed and direct as the chapter seems to suggest? Or is God's plan for each person more open-ended? Adventists have tended away from views of God that suggest every detail of our lives being overseen and controlled by Him. We have focused more on human freedom and the difference people can make in the fulfillment of God's goals for the world. The book of Job also tells us that some tragedies are so great that they may not seem to have a teaching purpose. So the thoughts in this chapter, as in many others, need to be applied in the context of "all other things being equal."

QUOTABLE QUOTES

"It is our own character and experience that determine our influence upon others. In order to convince others of the power of Christ's grace, we must know its power in our own hearts and lives. The gospel we present for the saving of souls must be the gospel by which our own souls are saved. Only through a living faith in Christ as a personal Saviour is it possible to make our influence felt in a skeptical world."

"By the power of His grace manifested in the transformation of character the world is to be convinced that God has sent His Son as its Redeemer. No other influence that can surround the human soul has such power as the influence of an unselfish life."

"To live such a life, to exert such an influence, costs at every step effort, self-sacrifice, discipline. It is because they do not understand this that many are so easily discouraged in the Christian life. Many who sincerely consecrate their lives to God's service are surprised and disappointed to find themselves, as never before, confronted by obstacles and beset by trials and perplexities. . . . Like Israel of old they question, 'If God is leading us, why do all these things come upon us?' "

"It is because God is leading them that these things come upon them. . . . He who reads the hearts of men knows their characters better than they themselves know them. He sees that some have powers and susceptibilities which, rightly directed, might be used in the advancement of His work. In His providence He brings these persons into different positions and varied circumstances that they may discover in their character the defects which have been concealed from their own knowledge. He gives them opportunity to correct these defects and to fit themselves for His service."

"Let us remember that while the work we have to do may not be our choice, it is to be accepted as God's choice for us. Whether pleasing or unpleasing, we are to do the duty that lies nearest."

"In the future life the mysteries that here have annoyed and disappointed us will be made plain. We shall see that our seemingly unanswered prayers and disappointed hopes have been among our greatest blessings."

"The Lord has no place in His work for those who have a greater desire to win the crown than to bear the cross. He wants men who are more intent upon doing their duty than upon receiving their reward—men who are more solicitous for principle than for promotion."

"Not by their wealth, their education, or their position does God estimate men. He estimates them by their purity of motive and their beauty of character. He looks to see how much of His Spirit they possess and how much of His likeness their life reveals. To be great in God's kingdom is to be as a little child in humility, in simplicity of faith, and in purity of love."

"Of all the gifts that heaven can bestow upon men, fellowship with Christ in His sufferings is the most weighty trust and the highest honor. Not Enoch, who was translated to heaven, not Elijah, who ascended in a chariot of fire, was greater or more honored than John the Baptist, who perished alone in the dungeon."

"Too many, in planning for a brilliant future, make an utter failure. Let God plan for you. As a little child, trust to the guidance of Him who will 'keep the feet of His saints.' 1 Samuel 2:9. God never leads His children otherwise than they would choose to be led, if they could see the end from the beginning and discern the glory of the purpose which they are fulfilling as co-workers with Him."

"Many who profess to be Christ's followers have an anxious, troubled heart because they are afraid to trust themselves with God. They do not make a complete surrender to Him, for they shrink from the consequences that such a surrender may involve. Unless they do make this surrender they cannot find peace."

"Our heavenly Father has a thousand ways to provide for us of which we know nothing. Those who accept the one principle of making the service of God supreme, will find perplexities vanish and a plain path before their feet."

@TWEETS_OF_HEALING

Thr is an eloquence far more #powerful than the eloquence of words in the quiet, consistent #life of a pure, true @Christian.

What a man is has more #influence than what he says.

It is our own character & exp that determine our influence upon others.

In order 2 convince others of the #power of @Christ's #grace, we must know its power in our own hearts & #lives.

The #gospel we present for the saving of #souls must b the gospel by which our own #souls r saved.

Only thru a living #faith in @Christ as a personal #Saviour is it possible 2 make our influence felt in a skeptical #world.

The strongest argument in favor of the #gospel is a loving & lovable @Christian.

#Trials & obstacles r the #Lord's chosen methods of discipline & #His appointed conditions of success.

The fact that we r called upon 2 endure #trial shows that @Jesus sees in us something #precious which He desires 2 develop.

Let us remember that whl the wrk we hve 2 do may not b our choice, it's 2 b accepted as @God's #choice for us.

Often our plans #fail that @God's plans for us may succeed.

In the future #life we will understand all the seemingly unanswered prayers & disappointed hopes.

The #Lord has no place in #His wrk for those who hve a gr8er desire 2 win the #crown than 2 bear the #cross.

Not by their wealth, #education, or position does @God estimate ppl bt by their purity of motive & beauty of #character.

To b gr8 in @God's kingdom is 2 b as a little #child in humility, in simplicity of #faith & in purity of #love.

Of all the gifts that #heaven cn bestow, fellowship wt @Christ in #His sufferings is the most weighty trust & highest honor.

Too many, in planning for a brilliant future, make an utter failure. Let @God plan for you.

Many who profess 2 b @Christ's followers hve an anxious, troubled heart because they r afraid 2 trust themselves wt @God.

Our #heavenly #Father has a thousand ways 2 provide for us of which we know nothng.

The faithful discharge of 2day's duties is the best preparation for tomorrow's #trials.

The only way for the #church 2 approach homosexuals is frm a standpoint of common brokenness, not out of a sense of superiority.

DISCUSSION QUESTIONS

1. When dealing with the sick and the dying, how and when is it appropriate to present the potential value that suffering can have in a person's life?
2. According to this chapter, in the future life we will understand all the seemingly unanswered prayers and disappointed hopes in this life. When and how should such a concept be shared with the sick and the dying?

IN CONTACT WITH OTHERS

CH. 41, PP. 483-496

SUMMARY

It is through personal relationships that Christianity comes in contact with the world. Everyone who has received the gospel is to share with those who are unacquainted with it. This chapter emphasizes the softer, gentler virtues of Christian faith: kindness, gentleness, patience, and sympathy. The focus is on the truth about life more than the truth about doctrine.

THOUGHTS

This chapter is a gold mine of counsel on relationships: how to deal with people who are contrary, difficult, or simply of a different opinion. Everyone is different, so those who wish to be successful in Christian relationships need to consider those differences and meet people where they are.

Among the qualities recommended in this chapter are patience and forbearance with leadership, avoiding hasty judgments regarding people's behavior and character, avoiding retaliation when wronged, presenting a positive attitude at all times, combining Christian graces with social justice, being faithful in the little things, being in control of one's thoughts and actions, speaking well of others, and being calm under provocation. While minds are quite varied, all are in need of kindness and sympathy.

This chapter is about more than just relationships. It has a strong focus on what we today would call "positive psychology." How we view ourselves has a strong impact on how we view others. On the other hand, an overwhelmingly positive attitude can sometimes come across as fake. In order to comply with this chapter, one may be tempted to bury feelings and needs to promote the right image. As always when it comes to Ellen White, it is important to approach her strongest statements with a sense of balance.

One challenging feature of this chapter is the concept that in times of crisis, we should turn to God alone. But in practice is God alone really enough for most people? When we lose a loved one to death, we truly miss them. God's presence can be a help, but the encouragement of others also makes a difference. *The Desire of Ages,* page 297, is a helpful balancing statement. There are people whose eyes are so blinded by tears that they cannot grasp the Unseen without the help of a visible companion.

An important concept in this chapter and also the New Testament (1 Pet. 3:9; Rom. 12) is that one should never retaliate. In the words of Paul Heubach, "Don't defend yourself. Your foes won't believe it and your friends don't need it."

QUOTABLE QUOTES

"Every association of life calls for the exercise of self-control, forbearance, and sympathy. We differ so widely in disposition, habits, education, that our ways of looking at things vary. We judge differently. Our understanding of truth, our ideas in regard to the conduct of life, are not in all respects the same. There are no two whose experience is alike in every particular. The trials of one are not the trials of another. The duties that one finds light are to another most difficult and perplexing."

"So frail, so ignorant, so liable to misconception is human nature, that each should be careful in the estimate he places upon another. We little know the bearing of our acts upon the experience of others. What we do or say may seem to us of little moment, when, could our eyes be opened, we should see that upon it depended the most important results for good or for evil."

"We cannot afford to let our spirits chafe over any real or supposed wrong done to ourselves. Self is the enemy we most need to fear. . . . No other

EVERYONE IS DIFFERENT, SO THOSE WHO WISH TO BE SUCCESSFUL IN CHRISTIAN RELATIONSHIPS NEED TO CONSIDER THOSE DIFFERENCES AND MEET PEOPLE WHERE THEY ARE.

victory we can gain will be so precious as the victory gained over self."

"We should not allow our feelings to be easily wounded. We are to live, not to guard our feelings or our reputation, but to save souls. As we become interested in the salvation of souls we cease to mind the little differences that so often arise in our association with one another. Whatever others may think of us or do to us, it need not disturb our oneness with Christ, the fellowship of the Spirit."

"If Christ dwells in us, we shall be patient, kind, and forbearing, cheerful amid frets and irritations. Day by day and year by year we shall conquer self, and grow into a noble heroism. This is our allotted task; but it cannot be accomplished without help from Jesus, resolute decision, unwavering purpose, continual watchfulness, and unceasing prayer."

"We need not keep our own record of trials and difficulties, griefs, and sorrows. All these things are written in the books, and heaven will take care of them. While we are counting up the disagreeable things, many things that are pleasant to reflect upon are passing from memory."

"If you do not feel lighthearted and joyous, do not talk of your feelings. Cast no shadow upon the lives of others. A cold, sunless religion never draws souls to Christ. . . . Instead of thinking of your discouragements, think of the power you can claim in Christ's name."

"When, notwithstanding disagreeable circumstances, we rest confidingly in His love, and shut ourselves in with Him, the sense of His presence will inspire a deep, tranquil joy."

"He who is imbued with the Spirit of Christ abides in Christ. Whatever comes to him comes from the Saviour, who surrounds him with His presence. Nothing can touch him except by the Lord's permission."

"The Lord Jesus demands our acknowledgment of the rights of every man. Men's social rights, and their rights as Christians, are to be taken into consideration. All are to be treated with refinement and delicacy, as the sons and daughters of God."

"Life is chiefly made up, not of great sacrifices and wonderful achievements, but of little things. . . . Only by acting upon principle in the tests of daily life can we acquire power to stand firm and faithful in the most dangerous and most difficult positions."

"The power of self-restraint strengthens by exercise. That which at first seems difficult, by constant repetition grows easy, until right thoughts and actions become habitual."

"Cultivate the habit of speaking well of others. Dwell upon the good qualities of those with whom you associate, and see as little as possible of their errors and failings. When tempted to complain of what someone has said or done, praise something in that person's life or character."

"Evilspeaking is a twofold curse, falling more heavily upon the speaker than upon the hearer. He who scatters the seeds of dissension and strife reaps in his own soul the deadly fruits. The very act of looking for evil in others develops evil in those who look. By dwelling upon the faults of others, we are changed into the same image."

"The consistent life, the patient forbearance, the spirit unruffled under provocation, is always the most conclusive argument and the most solemn appeal. If you have had opportunities and advantages that have not fallen to the lot of others, consider this, and be ever a wise, careful, gentle teacher."

"Until the judgment you will never know the influence of a kind, considerate course toward the inconsistent, the unreasonable, the unworthy. When we meet with ingratitude and betrayal of sacred trusts, we are roused to show our contempt or indignation. This the guilty expect; they are prepared for it. But kind forbearance takes them by surprise and often awakens their better impulses and arouses a longing for a nobler life."

@TWEETS_OF_HEALING

Every association of #life calls for the #exercise of self-control, forbearance & sympathy.

Thr r no two whose exp is alike in every particular.

Bitter exp gives us knowledge.

#Self is the #enemy we most need 2 fear.

We r 2 live, not 2 guard our feelings or our reputation, bt 2 save #souls.

Thr is wonderful #power in #silence.

If @Christ dwells in us, we shall b patient, kind & forbearing, cheerful amid frets & irritations.

Whl we r counting up the disagreeable things, many things that r pleasant 2 reflect upon r passing frm memory.

If u do not feel lighthearted & joyous, do not talk of ur feelings. Cast no shadow upon the #lives of others.

Instead of thinking of ur discouragements, think of the #power u cn claim in @Christ's name.

When we rest confidingly in #His #love, the sense of #His presence will inspire a deep, tranquil joy.

@Christ was courteous, even 2 his persecutors & #His true followers will manifest the same #spirit.

True refinement will nvr b revealed so long as self is considered as the supreme object.

#Life is chiefly made up, not of gr8 sacrifices & wonderful achievements, bt of little things.

The #power of self-restraint strengthens by #exercise.

The very act of looking for #evil in others develops evil in those who look.

#Evil speaking is a twofold #curse, falling more heavily upon the speaker than upon the hearer.

Regard yourselves as #missionaries, first of all, among ur fellow wrkers.

Until the #judgment u will nvr know the influence of a kind, considerate course toward the inconsistent, the unreasonable, the unworthy.

Whl #minds r quite varied, all r in need of #kindness & sympathy.

DISCUSSION QUESTIONS

1. What are some of your favorite counsels in the chapter regarding how to deal with the contrary and the difficult?
2. What are some qualities of character that are appropriate to every kind of situation and personality?

DEVELOPMENT AND SERVICE

CH. 42, PP. 497-502

SUMMARY

This chapter in many ways is the reverse focus of the previous one. Instead of gentleness, patience, and kindness, the character qualities emphasized here are courage, perseverance, and drive.

THOUGHTS

This chapter calls for the active virtues to be added to the more passive ones. Kindness and gentleness are at the core of Christian character, but it is things like courage and energy that overcome evil and provide power for good. Many accomplish little because they attempt little. Circumstances don't have to master us, we can master them. The sacrifice of Christ is ground enough for extra effort on our parts.

Many people find it easy for their personality to be smothered by the group. We want to please and when everyone else is going a certain way, it is easy to go along. But the cohesion of the group is often an illusion. Many are waiting for someone of courage to speak up. This chapter offers encouragement to live according to one's conscience, even though no one else seems to approve. This requires active strength of character that is grounded in a deep relationship with Christ.

QUOTABLE QUOTES

MANY ACCOMPLISH LITTLE BECAUSE THEY ATTEMPT LITTLE.

"Christian life is more than many take it to be. It does not consist wholly in gentleness, patience, meekness, and kindliness. These graces are essential; but there is need also of courage, force, energy, and perseverance. The path that Christ marks out is a narrow, self-denying path. To enter that path and press on through difficulties and discouragements requires men who are more than weaklings."

"Some who engage in missionary service are weak, nerveless, spiritless, easily discouraged. They lack push. They have not those positive traits of character that give power to do something—the spirit and energy that kindle enthusiasm. Those who would win success must be courageous and hopeful. They should cultivate not only the passive but the active virtues. While they are to give the soft answer that turns away wrath, they must possess the courage of a hero to resist evil. With the charity that endures all things, they need the force of character that will make their influence a positive power."

"Many who are qualified to do excellent work accomplish little because they attempt little. Thousands pass through life as if they had no great object for which to live, no high standard to reach. One reason for this is the low estimate which they place upon themselves. Christ paid an infinite price for us, and according to the price paid He desires us to value ourselves."

"Never think that you have learned enough, and that you may now relax your efforts. The cultivated mind is the measure of the man. Your education should continue during your lifetime; every day you should be learning and putting to practical use the knowledge gained."

"Everyone who accepts Christ as his personal Saviour will long for the privilege of serving God. Contemplating what heaven has done for him, his heart is moved with boundless love and adoring gratitude. He is eager to signalize his gratitude by devoting his abilities to God's service. He longs to show his love for Christ and for His purchased possession. He covets toil, hardship, sacrifice."

@TWEETS_OF_HEALING

Gentleness, patience, meekness & kindliness r essential; bt thr is need also of courage, force, energy & perseverance.

We r called 2 give the soft answer that turns away wrath, whl possessing the courage of a hero 2 resist #evil.

Your #education should continue during ur #lifetime; every day u should b #learning & putting 2 practical use the #knowledge gained.

Man cn shape circumstances, bt circumstances should not b allowed 2 shape the #man.

If #men cld b led 2 consider the amazing #sacrifice made by the #Majesty of #heaven, selfishness would b banished frm their #hearts.

Many accomplish little because they attempt little. They attempt little because of the low estimate they place upon themselves.

DISCUSSION QUESTIONS

1. This chapter balances the need for gentleness, patience, and kindness with the more active qualities of courage and the energy to overcome evil. How can we balance these two types of virtues in everyday life?
2. According to this chapter, what are the necessary prerequisites for a high sense of self-worth?

SUMMARY

We need daily a fresh revelation of Christ and continual progress in knowledge and virtue. The purpose of spiritual development is to more and more clearly express the character of God in the life, and to be more and more effective in service to others.

THOUGHTS

This is one of many chapters in *The Ministry of Healing* that has a very singular focus by design. Such chapters should not be absorbed in isolation, but need to be read within the larger context of surrounding chapters. Read in isolation, this chapter promotes a pietistic, experience-based approach to the spiritual life. Unless one feels the presence of God, one hasn't truly connected or perhaps even been redeemed. But this needs to be balanced with other statements. The reality is, spiritual life in most cases is quite mundane, learning to see God in the ordinary tasks of every day life, learning to see Jesus in the neighbor, the stranger, or the difficult child. In contrast, many programs of spiritual training emphasize the seeking of a "high" that is achievable during retreats but rarely lasts long during the work week. The following should be read with the above in mind.

The Holy Spirit works with those who are willing to be molded. If we are teachable and changeable, we can have a higher and deeper experience than we now know.

THE HOLY SPIRIT WORKS WITH THOSE WHO ARE WILLING TO BE MOLDED.

In a real sense, the last chapter of *The Ministry of Healing* reads like a meditation on John 15 in particular but also on Philippians 2 and the seven churches of Revelation.

A great motivation toward a higher experience is to meditate on the visions of future glory in books like Revelation. Another motivation is the "mountain-top experience" illustrated in the lives of Moses and the disciples of Jesus.

We can have that mountain-top experience when we are diligent and persevering in prayer. Christ sends messages to those who are willing to listen for His voice. The key to our defense against Satan's wiles is the continual exercise of prayer and faith combined with action. God's peace in the heart is what gives our words persuasive power.

When we are humble, contrite, and trust deeply in God, He can and will manifest Himself to us. Bible reading and the hearing of sermons will only help us if we put it to use in our practical everyday experience.

Given the important place this chapter fills at the close of *The Ministry of Healing*, it is interesting that so many Adventists today are leery of spiritual formation (the right kind, as the Seminary has taught for decades). The earliest Adventists, including Ellen White, were quite charismatic when it came to conversion and spiritual life. Although Ellen White became more formal by the 1860s, most Adventists remained very experiential in their faith right up to about 1900. Then reaction to the "holy flesh" movement and the intellectual concerns of the Fundamentalism/Modernism controversy seem to have diminished the focus on experiential faith that is so central to this chapter.

For Ellen White in this chapter, the "higher experience" is more about character development and effectiveness in service than it is doctrinal accuracy (though she would not want to leave the latter undone).

QUOTABLE QUOTES

"We need constantly a fresh revelation of Christ, a daily experience that harmonizes with His teachings. High and holy attainments are within our reach. Continual progress in knowledge and virtue is God's purpose for us. . . . Every day we may advance in perfection of Christian character."

"Those who are engaged in service for the Master need an experience much higher, deeper, broader, than many have yet thought of having. . . . Let these cherish every desire of the soul after God. The Holy Spirit works with those who will be worked, molds those who will be molded, fashions those who will be fashioned."

"We need to keep ever before us this vision of things unseen. It is thus that we shall be able to set a right value on the things of eternity and the things of time. It is this that will give us power to influence others for the higher life."

"Prayer and faith will do what no power on earth can accomplish. We are seldom, in all respects, placed in the same position twice. We continually have new scenes and new trials to pass through, where past experience cannot be a sufficient guide. We must have the continual light that comes from God."

"When we permit our communion with God to be broken, our defense is departed from us. Not all your good purposes and good intentions will enable you to withstand evil. . . . It is not always necessary to bow upon your knees in order to pray. Cultivate the habit of talking with the Saviour when you are alone, when you are walking, and when you are busy with your daily labor. Let the heart be continually uplifted in silent petition for help, for light, for strength, for knowledge. Let every breath be a prayer."

"Nothing is more needed in our work than the practical results of communion with God. We should show by our daily lives that we have peace and rest in the Saviour. His peace in the heart will shine forth in the countenance. It will give to the voice a persuasive power. . . . This will impart to the worker a power that nothing else can give. Of this power he must not allow himself to be deprived."

"If you had the greatest intellect ever given to man, it would not be sufficient for your work. . . . The result of all we do rests in the hands of God."

"When we are humble and contrite we stand where God can and will manifest Himself to us. He is well pleased when we urge past mercies and blessings as a reason why He should bestow on us greater blessings. He will more than fulfill the expectations of those who trust fully in Him. The Lord Jesus . . . bestows upon us all that we will employ in blessing others and ennobling our own souls."

"We must have less trust in what we ourselves can do, and more trust in what the Lord can do for and through us. You are not engaged in your own work; you are doing the work of God. Surrender your will and way to Him. Make not a single reserve, not a single compromise with self. Know what it is to be free in Christ."

"The mere hearing of sermons Sabbath after Sabbath, the reading of the Bible through and through, or the explanation of it verse by verse, will not benefit us or those who hear us, unless we bring the truths of the Bible into our individual experience. The understanding, the will, the affections, must be yielded to the control of the word of God. Then through the work of the Holy Spirit the precepts of the word will become the principles of the life."

"Walk continually in the light of God. Meditate day and night upon His character. Then you will see His beauty and rejoice in His goodness. Your heart will glow with a sense of His love. You will be uplifted as if borne by everlasting arms. With the power and light that God imparts, you can comprehend more and accomplish more than you ever before deemed possible."

@TWEETS_OF_HEALING

Continual progress in #knowledge & virtue is @God's purpose for us.

Prayer & faith will do what no #power on earth cn accomplish.

When we permit our communion wt @God 2 b broken, our defense is departed frm us.

Let every breath b a #prayer.

Nothng is more needed in our wrk than the practical results of communion wt @God.

We must live a two-fold life–a #life of thought & action, of silent #prayer & earnest wrk.

If u had the gr8est intellect ever given 2 man, it would not b sufficient for ur wrk.

When we r humble & contrite we stand where @God cn & will manifest #Himself 2 us.

We must hve less #trust in what we ourselves cn do & more trust in what the #Lord cn do for & thru us.

Walk continually in the #light of @God.

DISCUSSION QUESTIONS

1. According to this chapter, what are the keys to having a "mountain-top" kind of experience with God?
2. What do chapters 40–43 tell us about God?

NOTES

NOTES

NOTES

NOTES

NOTES

NOTES

NOTES

NOTES